Praise for *Employing the Enemy*

'Vickery convincingly illuminates a little known aspect of Israel's occupation of the West Bank – the exploitation and abuse of Palestinians so desperate for work that they take underpaid and humiliating jobs in Israeli settlements.'

Richard Falk, former UN Special Rapporteur
on Palestinian rights

'Provides a vivid exposition of the material struggles and moral dilemmas faced by these workers, as well as the ways in which their labour produces its own small, steadfast gestures of resistance.'

John Reynolds, author of *Empire, Emergency
and International Law*

'The story of Palestinian workers in Israeli settlements is not well known. This book tells it with candour and vividness. Essential reading for those who want to understand the true extent of Israel's domination of the Palestinians.'

Ghada Karmi, author of *Return:
A Palestinian Memoir*

'A forensic and humane study of Palestinian workers in Israeli settlements, Vickery's book is a much-needed resource on a complex issue.'

Ben White, author of *Israeli Apartheid:
A Beginner's Guide*

About the Author

MATTHEW VICKERY is a journalist and researcher covering conflict, human rights, and workers' rights issues throughout the Middle East, as well as extensively in Israel and the occupied Palestinian territories. His bylines include *Al-Jazeera*, *Foreign Policy*, *Ha'aretz*, *The Times*, and *USA Today* among others.

EMPLOYING THE ENEMY

The Story of Palestinian Labourers on Israeli Settlements

MATTHEW VICKERY

ZED
Zed Books
London

Employing the Enemy: The Story of Palestinian Labourers on Israeli Settlements
was first published in 2017 by Zed Books Ltd, The Foundry, 17 Oval Way,
London SE11 5RR, UK.

www.zedbooks.net

Typeset in Bulmer by Swales and Willis Ltd, Exeter, Devon
Index by ed.emery@thefreeuniversity.net
Cover design by Clare Turner
Cover photo © Andrew McConnell/Panos

A catalogue record for this book is available from the British Library.

ISBN 978-1-78360-995-6 hb
ISBN 978-1-78360-994-9 pb
ISBN 978-1-78360-996-3 pdf
ISBN 978-1-78360-997-0 epub
ISBN 978-1-78360-998-7 mobi

Printed and bound by CPI Group (UK) Ltd, Croydon, CR0 4YY

Contents

Acknowledgements

My thanks must be extended firstly, and most importantly, to the many workers I sat down with, who welcomed me into their homes, and let me into their personal and work lives. Workers who chose to talk about their work, despite risks to their employment if found out. That took a level of courage that I am not just thankful for, but that I admire greatly. Workers who wanted to set the record straight, who wanted to explain to those looking in from the outside that the reality is not as simple as it may seem, that it is complex, and that it damages them. To Ali, Hamza, and Mahmoud, those thanks are furthered even more, for going above and beyond.

Thanks to the team at Kav LaOved who, for several years now, have selflessly helped with this project and others, and who themselves do tireless and important workers' rights advocacy. Abed, Angie, Nirit, Noa, and Taghrid, deserve special thanks. My thanks to Human Rights Watch, MAAN Development Center and WAC-MAAN, whose staff have given much help for the duration of this project. Hamza Zubeidat, in particular for his help and his inspiring advocacy work for workers and human rights causes in the Jordan Valley.

My thanks to Kim Walker and the team at Zed Books for their hard work and encouragement, and to Professor Ilan Pappe whose guidance and encouragement at Exeter University several years ago was the starting point for this project. My deep gratitude also to Hector MacKenzie who played a pivotal role in making this book happen.

Thanks to Harry, Jagoda, Julie, Marta and Satu for your invaluable feedback and to Abed and Sheren for your help in getting this project to this point. Thanks as well to my family for their continued support during my career.

Lastly, to my Palestinian friends in both Gaza and the West Bank, as well as around the world, who continue to show strength, steadfastness and humour, despite continued occupation. Thank you for educating and teaching me over the years and letting me into your homes and welcoming me into your country. I hope this book in some small part does your struggle justice.

Introduction

It seems like a political contradiction at first, the presence of thousands of Palestinian workers queuing up outside the illegal Israeli settlements at the crack of dawn. All ready for a hard day's work toiling in the very facts on the ground that continue to entrench occupation and bring so much hardship and grief to the West Bank Palestinian population. It seems even more of a harmful contradiction when some of those workers are construction workers, literally building and expanding the settlements with their own hands. The settlements have transformed the West Bank, splitting the Palestinian territory into pieces, impacting negatively and devastatingly on Palestinian lives. They are omnipresent everywhere, often perched on top of the West Bank's rolling hills, looking down on the much poorer and heavily occupied Palestinian population below. It is no coincidence, however, that the settlements, deemed illegal under international law, sit above Palestinian towns and villages. Israel's settlement project may be driven by Zionist ideology, but its conception on the ground is very much strategic in regards to controlling the Palestinian population; splitting it up into easily controllable groups. In the West Bank 'bantustans' – unconnected ethnically homogenous (Palestinian) enclaves that are not sovereign and are fundamentally controlled by Israel – have been purposefully created.

The settlements are not just hubs of ideological settlers any more. Most seamlessly merge into the Israeli state through an extensive infrastructure network that connects the settlements to major Israeli cities, turning those settlements into commuter towns, as well as fully functioning economies themselves with factories, farms, and other industry. These businesses all attempt to bring a cloak of legitimacy and normality to what are communities that are illegal under international law, and that have been built on stolen Palestinian land, and continue to be sustained through Palestinian resources. If the average consumer purchases products that originate from the settlements or uses a settlement company's services, and then wishes to question the contradiction of Palestinians working in and in turn bolstering the settlements, at a quick glance they will easily find rhetoric from companies and the Israeli government claiming that settlement employment is a highly positive thing. It's not unusual to find a settlement worker that has been quoted by an Israeli newspaper in a positive news article about settlement work. Settlement companies and Israeli politicians say those who oppose the settlements and support the Boycott, Divestment and Sanctions (BDS) movement, are damaging workers by being against entities (the settlements) that provide employment and a wage to Palestinians. Yet this is the rhetoric of the occupier, and of the dominant and loudest narrative. If you travel to the rural West Bank villages where many Palestinian settlement workers are from, sit down in their homes, and talk about their lives and work, a different picture emerges. These workers talk of dangerous conditions, of life-altering injuries, of being paid well below the legal Israeli minimum wage (which they are entitled to), and being subjected to humiliating and threatening treatment at the hands of their employers, unscrupulous middlemen, and Israeli soldiers. Their communities are poverty-stricken, and the lives these villagers used to live before occupation, one where an income came from farming and herding, has been destroyed through no fault of their own. The land has been stripped from them and literally annexed from under their feet, and the settlements have landed, unwanted, and with disastrous consequences at their doorstep.

Area C – where these rural Palestinian communities are mainly situated, an area under full Israeli administrative and military control that takes up more than 60 percent of the West Bank – has four times more settlers than Palestinians living there. This area, which is resource rich, and should be the economic and development hub of any Palestinian state, has been purposefully stifled by Israeli policy, as Israel has looked to limit Palestinian development and keep its economy weak, while using those very resources – the fertile land, water, and minerals – for the benefit of the Israeli population and in direct opposition to international law. Crucially, Israeli policy has also sought to exploit another of the West Bank's resources; its vulnerable, easily exploitable, and impoverished rural workforce. This is why there are twenty settlement industrial zones and hundreds of Israeli factories, along with dozens of agricultural settlements that cultivate over 9,000 hectares of occupied West Bank land. These workers are paid sometimes as little as 30–40 percent of the legal minimum wage a day, while some who have to carry out the back-breaking and often hazardous work in the agricultural settlements are children as young as 12 years-old. Settlement work is not welcome, but it has become a necessity to survive where no other options exist. "We have no other choice," are the words that are echoed up and down the rural villages that sit in the valleys of the West Bank, often towered from above by large, imposing settlements, with their heavily armed civilian and soldier presence.

There are roughly 20,000–30,000 Palestinians working legally in the settlements at one time, but several thousand more work illegally without Israeli governmental permission, taking the dangerous journey on foot under the cover of darkness, sneaking into the settlements before dawn unnoticed. A few years ago with the guidance of a friend, I did one of these illegal routes myself. It was a short one, took less than an hour and took us from Palestinian controlled areas, up a hill, dodging and hiding from a patrolling Israeli army jeep on one of the military roads surrounding a settlement, and then hugging a forest, into that settlement. It was surprisingly easy, in fact much easier than travelling to some Palestinian areas in the West Bank. That is, of course, not to undermine the risks that routes such as these have for Palestinian workers, especially those workers' routes that involve directly climbing over the Wall, and running past Israeli military watchtowers. Workers can be fatally shot if seen by soldiers, and arrested and jailed if caught. What taking this route illustrated to me, however, were two important things. The first was that settlement work is seemingly more accessible to some unemployed Palestinians – especially those from rural areas that sit beside the settlements – than travelling for work in Palestinian Authority areas. The freedom of movement restrictions imposed by Israel between Palestinian populated areas can be that severe. The second was that the risk these workers had to take was not just substantial, but also routine. It exists every time they make the journey. To do this week in, week out, there *must* be a level of economic desperation for thousands of workers to undertake such a risky journey with such frequency.

The Israeli government, and settlement employers themselves, would like the outsider to believe that the phenomenon of Palestinians working in the settlements is a positive one, that shows Israelis as lending a helping hand, giving a wage, and improving the lives of their occupied and impoverished counterparts. This rosy image is one that may make an individual believe that such work fosters co-operation and is a beacon of hope in a stagnant, seven-decade-long conflict, and therefore should be encouraged. Yet as important as it is to find positives in such a situation, settlement employment in its current form is not this. If anything, settlement employment of West Bank Palestinians shows the depressing nature of Israel's occupation of Palestinian land and lives in its truest colours. This book is an attempt to show that nature. For those workers that tilled the land before occupation in 1967, and in the initial years following, when the settlements were fewer and smaller in size, a dependency on the Israeli labour market grew over the years as their land was taken from them. Israeli control strengthened, freedom of movement became more restricted as more checkpoints sprang up and the construction of the Wall begun. Working in the settlements became the only viable income stream for thousands. Settlement employers gained a cheap workforce, desperate for an income, and exploited that workforce with impunity. The path to settlement employment isn't a free choice; Israeli policy past and present has created the current situation, and forced workers into a unique and depressing reality – to survive, to put food on the table and look after their family, requires bolstering the settlements and boosting the profit of their occupiers. Settlement employers may be employing and paying their 'enemy' but the only reason for this is profit, while the Israeli government continues year-on-year to encourage the exploitation of this Palestinian workforce as an added benefit of a devastating and immoral occupation.

PART I

Employing the 'Enemy'

ONE | Employing the 'Enemy'

"Hurry, it's cold!" the rushed voice of Mahmoud bellows from the front door of his small but cosy ground-level home. It's one of those rare snowy winter days in Palestine when Mahmoud appears suddenly at his door in Al-Walaja village. It's not a day to spend prolonged periods of time outside, and as is the nature of Palestinian hospitality, Mahmoud didn't intend on letting anyone meander through his village, stranger or not, as snow began to fall. Inside his home, his three young kids wander the modest house, eventually gravitating towards the wood burner that Mahmoud and his two brothers huddle around. It's a Tuesday, but it's a day off for the men. The weather – wet, cold, windy, and with a good amount of snow – has ensured they won't be working on their building sites today.

"You know, I don't feel good. Working there I mean," Mahmoud[1] says as he lays out a typical breakfast of hummus, falafel, freshly baked bread, thyme, and olives, in front of the wood burner. "Knowing you are building their state. You are helping them. But at the same time, you are forced to do this, if you don't do this, you can't survive."

Mahmoud has spent the last few years working as a labourer, almost exclusively as a construction worker in Israel's illegal settlements in the West Bank. His brothers are the same. He earns

140 NIS ($36) for eight hours work a day? – it's nowhere near enough by law. The Israeli minimum wage stands at 25 NIS an hour ($6.50), or for a full day's work, a minimum of 214.62 NIS ($56.50).[3] Israeli law states clearly that all workers in the settlements, including the estimated thirty to forty thousand West Bank Palestinians who work there, are entitled to that minimum wage.[4] But Mahmoud's illegal underpayment is not an exception. Settler employers routinely ignore the rights of Palestinian workers that are enshrined in Israeli labour law.

"It's the only way"
"There is no other option for us," Mahmoud sighs. He knows it looks like a contradiction to an outsider, a Palestinian working, and in turn bolstering, creating, and expanding the illegal Israeli settlements. But for Mahmoud, there is no other way for him to survive. "They make the settlements, they took the land from us, and that takes away our livelihood," he says talking about the arable life that many Palestinian families forged a livelihood from before 1967 and the start of Israel's occupation of the West Bank. With occupation came the land grabs undertaken by the Israeli military, with much of the rural land annexed for the creation and later expansion of the settlements, as well as large military zones, areas in which Palestinians are forbidden to farm or even enter. The lifestyle of living off the land that Mahmoud's grandparents and parents had always known began to dwindle, until eventually as more and more land was taken over the years, it was no longer possible.

"They know they will get cheap workers because of this," Mahmoud says of Israel's land grabs and occupation. "If they come and take the land from a village, then they know the people will lose money, their income, their jobs, and so they will have to look at Israel to get work, to get money. They will need to do this to survive, it's the only way."

His two brothers who sit beside him nod in dejected agreement. They both work the nearby settlements of Beitar Illit, Gilo, Har Gilo, and Ma'ale Adumim, jumping between them depending on where work is available. One of them even works illegally without a work permit – the document from Israel's Civil Administration that authorises a Palestinian to legally enter a settlement and work there. If a soldier discovers a Palestinian in the settlements without one, they will be arrested and face imprisonment. "That's our life," Mahmoud's brother shrugs stoically, "I don't have any other choice."

At least 80 percent of Palestinian settlement workers are estimated to be paid less than minimum wage.[5] And that's just a conservative estimate. Illegal workers, especially, are almost always paid less. Making up between 15–30 percent of the overall Palestinian workforce in the settlements, their vulnerability from their known illegal status leaves them more susceptible to exploitation and blackmail from their employer (Alenat, 2010).

The journey to work for permit-holding legal workers can be demanding in its own right, involving long cramped queues outside settlement checkpoints at dawn under the scrutiny of fully armed Israeli soldiers who have been known to carry out humiliating treatment and searches on Palestinians passing through (B'Tselem, 2011; Sbeih, 2011). For an illegal worker, that journey is even more daunting. Dangerously crossing from Palestinian populated areas of the West Bank under the cover of darkness, and into the heavily guarded settlements, illegal workers risk being shot if sighted and/or imprisoned if caught by soldiers. It's an extreme risk that has resulted in deaths before (ILO, 2015: 24). However with a fifth of the population in poverty and an unemployment rate that tends to fluctuate around 15–20 percent in the West Bank, being able to feed your family and put food on the table takes precedence.

"We start gathering with other workers at 3am at [name of village removed], this isn't close to the work but it is the best place to cross the Wall," Mousa,[6] an illegal worker says of his risky journey to Ma'ale Adumim settlement where he works. The journey for Mousa begins as early as 3am in the morning. "We use a ladder and cross all at once, but before we cross we sit for half an hour looking out for soldiers or any movement, we need to make sure we are all alone. We make sure we know what is happening around us. Once we've got over the Wall, we hide under the trees for some time watching for the soldiers again. Then we have a two-hour walk through fields and mountains to the settlement. I'm always so scared of this journey. I feel lucky every time I make it safe."

If you know the right places and the right people, Palestinian workers can be seen stealthily making their way along known (in workers' circles anyway) routes such as the one Mousa takes. Some of those routes may require as much as ten miles of walking[7] in the pitch dark, over hills, valleys, and the Wall and its crisscrossing structure.[8] Some workers use ladders, others know small holes in the Wall's structure that they can crawl through,[9] avoiding any IDF jeeps that patrol the military roads surrounding the settlements as they go. It has become a dangerous routine for illegal Palestinian workers, but one borne out of necessity. Once inside a settlement, permit-less workers may stay there for days or weeks at a time, sleeping homeless on worksites to reduce the number of times they make the dangerous journey back and forth from their home to the settlement. Employers, aware that these workers are illegal and do not have the relevant permission and permits to be there, 'brutally violate the rights of workers who have no permits,' paying them even less and often making them work longer hours than other Palestinian settlement workers, aware that they can be exploited more easily than their permit-holding colleagues due to the constant threat of imprisonment that hangs over their heads (Kav LaOved, 2012: 36). Employers remorselessly use the permit system to their advantage (see Chapter 2). If workers have them, employers can threaten to have the permits revoked if they complain about pay or working conditions. For workers without, employers can alert the authorities to their illegal status at any time.

Mahmoud has a permit to work in the settlements, but permit or not, he says he would still find a way in. He's had to in the past, and he believes he will have to again in the future. But when you have a family to feed, risks such as illegal crossings have to be taken. Palestinians with permits like Mahmoud, and those without like his brother, often find themselves working side by side in the settlements. The former just happen to go through a checkpoint, the latter dodge soldiers and hike the hills under the cover of the early morning darkness.

Even if Palestinian settlement workers like Mahmoud find themselves working alongside Israelis in settlements while on the job, they shouldn't expect the same wage. Israeli workers in the same company and for the same tenure make more than double what their Palestinian colleagues earn (Bank of Israel, 2014). Discrimination against Palestinian workers is epidemic, where they are willingly treated as a cheap and disposable workforce by profiteering settlement employers. The human rights abuses undertaken by settlement businesses, through the exploitation of their Palestinian workers and the damage done from benefitting from the severe land grabs[10] and occupation, are so severe that Human Rights Watch has called on all businesses to "cease carrying out [their] activities" immediately (Human Rights Watch, 2016: 2).

A village of settlement workers

"These," Mahmoud says with pride in his voice, picking up the shiny green olives that sit center stage on the breakfast table "are the best olives in Palestine. They're from the land here in Al-Walaja. A gallon of oil from this land is worth 1,000 Shekels [NIS], from other areas it is about 500 to 600 Shekels. The land is very fertile but most of it has been stolen now by the Israelis, or if it has not been taken, we still can't harvest it, the soldiers won't let us go near it. They might shoot us, they can arrest us on our own land. You take the land from the people, and it makes the people weaker."

Al-Walaja, the rural village Mahmoud lives in, used to rely heavily on that fertile land. As a farming community, the residents live in a microcosm of what the Israeli occupation of Palestine really is. The villagers are refugees – not so unusual in the West Bank where a quarter of Palestinians are regarded as refugees by the UNRWA – but the refugees of Al-Walaja can actually see their former home from their doorstep every day. On top of an adjacent hill, clearly visible from Mahmoud's house, are the homes and land of old Al-Walaja. The Palestinians of the village fled in 1948 during the Arab-Israeli war, but many didn't go far expecting a quick resolution to the violence and a swift return to their homes. When that outcome began to look unlikely, the villagers of Al-Walaja started to rebuild again. They created their village for a second time, named it Al-Walaja in homage to their now taken hometown, and began farming the land. Life was hard, but possible. The land was fertile, becoming renowned for olives, apricots, and grapes. Animals roamed and grazed the hills, and provided an income to a resourceful and industrious village of refugees.

After Israel's swift and decisive capture of the West Bank from Jordanian forces in the 1967 Six-Day War and the subsequent Israeli occupation, the situation began to worsen again. Settlement outposts sprung up on the hills with government encouragement,[11] starting small, but as the years passed they grew bigger as the government financed new housing units, connected the settlements to water and electricity networks, and built an extensive road network that incorporated them into the very fabric of the Israeli state.[12] Much of the land farmed by the refugees of Al-Walaja was stripped from them to ensure the continued growth of surrounding Gilo and Har Gilo settlements. With the building of the Wall in 2002 during the *Second Intifada*, even more land was taken.[13] Snaking through the West Bank, the Wall annexed large swathes of Palestinian land incorporating much of it into the settlements that ran along its path. Al-Walaja was left in the *seam zone*, an enclave of land stuck on the 'Israeli' side of the Wall. The Wall may not lie between old and new Al-Walaja villages, but that land between is still a no-go zone for Palestinians living here. Much of the limited land left to cultivate – agricultural terraces painstakingly built by residents into the hill where Al-Walaja sits – has been scheduled to be turned into a nature reserve by the Israeli government, destroying what little crops and grazing land Al-Walaja residents had left. It's just the annexation of more Palestinian land, yet under the friendly sounding and easy-to-support idea of 'land preservation.' The eye-pleasing terraces creation and decades-long cultivation by the residents of the village have become their downfall. For residents to even protest such a decision requires an appeal with the Israel Land Authority at their office in Jerusalem. Yet very few residents have the needed permits to cross into Israel and launch an appeal[14] – it's a tactic the government have used since the beginning of the occupation in order to annex more land with very little or no legal backlash. It's the sort of Kafkaesque reality that has made up the lives of residents in Al-Walaja for decades. The village's depressing reality is also a perfect example of how occupation has created a situation where Palestinians have found themselves working as cheap labour for their occupiers. Loss of land, livelihood, high unemployment rates and restrictions on freedom of movement, has resulted in the oxymoron of Palestinians working and building the very settlements that continue that harsh reality. Livelihoods were lost and work in the Israeli labour market became the only source of income for many.[15] They didn't choose the work; it literally came to their doorstep and forced itself on them through economic necessity. Replace the name Al-Walaja with Al-Jiflik, the impoverished Bedouin community in the Jordan Valley, and it's a similar story. Or with Nil'in in Ramallah governorate, or Majdal Bani Fadel or Nahalin or Qabalan. There are towns like Al-Walaja all over the West Bank.

Driving around the village in a beat-up grey Volvo driven by Mahmoud's cousin Ali, Mahmoud starts to point out passing houses. "This man works in a supermarket in one of the settlements," he says, the car turning a corner and descending down one of the hilly roads. "And this one, in construction," motioning towards another house a few meters down the hill. In a five minute drive around the village, the Wall has been driven alongside, imposing Israeli military towers passed with armed soldiers on guard, masses of annexed land seen but forbidden to go near, and the houses of electricians, builders, painters, and supermarket workers – all working in the settlements – pointed out. Settlement work is an unfortunate, yet necessary, village affair.

Parking outside a small one-level home in the center of the village, the slight smell of apple can be discerned from the cold sharp air. "Can you smell the argila from here?" Mahmoud says of the scent as he approaches the door of 21-year-old Mohammed, a handyman who does odd jobs in the bustling 50,000 strong settlement of Beitar Illit. "He just works and smokes, works and smokes," he says joking about the argila addiction of the family, the popular tobacco water pipe that can be found in most Palestinian homes.

Mohammed[16] and his father wear warm welcoming smiles that hide the dire financial situation that the family worries about every day. Mohammed is the only one employed in the family of five – money isn't just a constant worry, getting food on the table is too. Still, extended family members try and help out where they can, and seem to always provide a bit of tobacco for the family argila addiction, their way to de-stress. In the bare living room, the slight smell of apple argila smoke has turned noticeably stronger, wafting round the concrete walls and floor. A small oil burner sits in the center of the room. It gives off some heat but the room is still freezing. Sugary Arabic tea is produced within minutes, such hospitality is customary but the tea almost appears to be used more as a way to keep the hands warm rather than as something to drink.

Mohammed doesn't open up quickly about his work. There's still a level of hostility against settlement workers – even in Al-Walaja where work in the settlements and Israel has been the biggest employment sector for years (ARIJ, 2010a). More wealthy families who have the luxury of owning their own business, or who have kept the majority of their land intact, sometimes brand the workers as traitors against Palestine, Mohammed says. Palestinians living in the large West Bank cities like Bethlehem, Ramallah, Hebron, and Nablus, who had less reliance on the land to make a living, and where there is a significantly smaller population of residents who are employed in the Israeli labour market,[17] are also prone to using such terminology. While working in Israel is seen as acceptable in general, as it does not aid the settlements directly, settlement work is not, and is subject to a Palestinian Authority (PA) ban – albeit a ban that has never actually been enforced (see Chapter 5). Settlements, understandably and with good reason, are seen by Palestinian society and the PA government as wholly illegitimate and the biggest obstacle to ending occupation. Ask the refugees in Al-Balata refugee camp in Nablus about settlement workers and many will tell you they are traitors for the Palestinian cause, or on the streets of bustling Hebron, and city residents will tell you they look down on them for being against Palestine. But ask Fadi,[18] a settlement worker in Ariel, and he will tell you, "there is nothing I can do"; or Aymad[19] who says, "The work feels like the work of a slave"; or Khader[20] who will tell you he feels "sadness and hurt to be working [in the settlement], but this is the only way to get food for my children."

Mohammed, 21 years old, has similar sentiments. "I'm upset about working in the settlements. If I could find a job in the Palestinian Authority areas then I would stop," he says grasping the hot tea tightly in his right hand. "If I had a chance to start my own business, build a project, I would do it. But it's Area C here [the area of the West Bank under complete Israeli military control]. I can't create anything. We have to get permission from the Israelis to do that. And that's impossible."

"He's right," Mahmoud interjects. "My uncle and neighbour tried to make a chicken farm so they could work for themselves, but because it was in Area C the Israeli government destroyed it. To make your own business here, in this village, it is difficult. It's a big risk."

Mohammed nods in agreement. "People are afraid to start businesses, and make projects like this. You would have to spend what little money you had or saved, and it will probably be for nothing. The Israeli army would just come and destroy it. If you have connections with Israeli businessmen then maybe it can be done."

Area C encompasses 60 percent of the total area of the West Bank and is under full Israeli military control.[21] Permission to build anything, even if it's just a small chicken coop on your own land, has to go through Israel. Almost every Palestinian application to build or develop on Area C land is rejected. Only a miniscule 1.5–3 percent are approved per year (OCHA, 2016). If a structure is built regardless, it's usually a matter of time before Caterpillar bulldozers contracted out by the Israeli government and flanked by army jeeps and soldiers, come and destroy it.

Mohammed makes 120 NIS a day for an eight-hour shift. He knows that by law he should earn nearly double that, but he doesn't dare ask for more. Although settlement work remains somewhat taboo, with unemployment so high in the West Bank – particularly for under 30s like himself – a job is still a job, and he knows that with so many of his peers in a dire financial situation and desperately needing money, his employer wouldn't hesitate to fire him if he asked for a raise or complained. Employers know that for every worker they have, there are thousands more just like them waiting in the wings for any work they can get.

Mohammed's mother, Namer, a kind-hearted middle-aged women, who insists on ensuring everyone in her company is always well-catered for, has a constant look of worry on her face as her son speaks. "I'm so worried about him," she says joining the conversation. "He could get killed."

The settlements, heavily guarded by Israeli soldiers and armed security guards, as well as a civilian population that has been encouraged by high-ranking Israeli officials to carry arms (Kaplan, 2015), means Namer worries that with every escalation in violence in the Israel/Palestine conflict, her son could end up being the victim of a nervous, trigger happy soldier or settler. Mohammed has strict orders from his parents to keep his head down, work hard, be quiet, and not question orders. "There's no choice but for him to work there," she laments. "If we need gas to heat the home then we need money. His father is ill, he has a problem with the discs in his back. His two brothers are unemployed, we need to have bread for the table. Life is expensive. He has to work there."

There is an air of guilt for working in the settlements, but also desperation from Mohammed. With his family to cater for, he doesn't see any alternative to the meager income he earns working in the very *facts on the ground*, as the settlements have been aptly termed, that are the lifeblood of Israel's occupation and control of the West Bank, and that continue to stymie the self-determination aspirations of Palestinians like himself. "If I had a choice I would stop working there," he says dejectedly. "But I don't."

TWO | The middleman and the power of the permit

It's still snowing on and off on another cold day in Palestine when Abed appears at the door of his lavish home on the outskirts of Bethlehem. Unlike other Palestinians that work in the settlements, Abed's home oozes disposable income. Garish, over-embellished gold-coloured ornaments are placed around his spacious living room. Five well looked after antique-esque couches flank the walls of the room, leaving a large open square of space in the middle as though in an attempt to show off the excess and unneeded square meters on show.

Abed, in his early 50s, is a middleman – the elusive and notorious characters that act as unscrupulous brokers between settlement employers and Palestinian workers, effectively forging the working and exploitative relationship between both. Middlemen like Abed claim they are helping Palestinians gain jobs by providing them with the easiest route to employment in the settlements – directly sorting the employment terms and payment out with the settler employer on behalf of workers. After all, to work as a middleman you must already have access to employers, speak Hebrew to communicate effectively, and know the ins and outs of the settlement employment sector. They are a route into employment for an estimated 30 to 50 percent of Palestinians employed in the settlements, those workers who do not already have the connections (previous employers, or family members already working in the settlements) to get a job themselves. Many workers not using a middleman usually started out with one. Yet middlemen are a poisoned chalice. Their very existence acts as a safety net for employers to exploit their workforce more easily by creating blurred lines in the whole employment process. It's why using middlemen has become an increasingly common practice for employers over the past two decades. "They [settlement employers] know exactly the ways to avoid the law," Abed[1] says matter-of-factly. And he should know, he's one of those ways.

Middlemen hold high societal status in their hometowns and have large and powerful extended families; it's why employers often pick them for the role in the first place. Their authority is not easy to question for workers who rely directly on them not just for their job but also to sort out a work permit, a document that only an employer has the power to ask the relevant Israeli authorities for. The permit is, for many, a golden ticket to employment and crucially one that allows a worker to go through the relative safety of an Israeli army checkpoint, rather than crossing illegally and risk being shot and/or imprisoned. It's a document that workers often fear losing more than their job – a permit could, at least, be a potential gateway to replacement employment. If it's revoked then they're not just thrown back into the pool of unemployed workers with thousands of others, they also find themselves permit-less and back at the bottom of the queue.

That fear of having a permit rescinded is something employers wield often to control their workforce, keep them in line, and use as a bargaining chip if a worker threatens to go to court (Alenat, 2010). There have been frequent cases where employers have threatened workers with not just removing their permit, but getting them "blacklisted" (Kav LaOved, 2012: 14) – a permanent ban from working in Israel or the settlements, a status usually reserved for Palestinians who have spent an extended amount of time in an Israeli prison. It's not just a threat. Employers have been known to alert security officials to certain workers and fabricate security concerns about them because they were being vocal about their rights (Human Rights Watch, 2016: 97). One Palestinian lawyer who represents workers in the settlements even discovered that every worker who had come to him to launch a case against an employer had then consequently been blacklisted from all Israeli settlements by that employer. In some cases relatives of those who had complained had also been fired and blacklisted.[2] It's a bargaining chip that middlemen are happy to wield as they play the role of enforcer and executor. They hire workers who they think won't cause a problem, will not ask for the legal minimum wage, for a raise, or be vocal about working conditions or rights they are entitled to.[3] Just like the employer, middlemen don't want to hear any talk of unionisation or workers' rights. If a worker is being too vocal, they can, and will, fire them and replace them with ease. Jobs are extremely limited compared to the high demand and need for them, while finding workers could not be easier. Unemployed workers even use so called "labour markets," (Kav LaOved, 2012: 13) where they will gather – for example at settlement checkpoints in the early morning – in the hope of running into a middleman and gaining work for the day. No contracts are signed. Workers are just picked up and go.

Ultimately the middleman's purpose is to avoid as much documentation and communication between worker and employer as possible – protecting the latter from accusations of workers' rights abuses through any form of paper trail. After all, if no contract

exists because the contracting of workers has been outsourced, an
employer can claim ignorance on the matter. While some employers may fake the documents they produce so they look legal and
legitimate,[4] using a middleman means an employer doesn't necessarily have to acknowledge some of the workers even exist. It
also helps employers to pay workers in cash, via a middleman,
reducing the paper trail of pay slips and working hours that could
go against them if a case made it to court. The middleman is, in
essence, a buffer between the worker and employer, but also, from
legal ramifications of exploitation. They've been aptly described
by Hussain Foqha,[5] the director of the Palestinian General Federation of Trade Unions (PGFTU) as "players of the law," who
are unscrupulous in their dealings with workers.

While not giving workers pay slips and contracts are now common tactics amongst settlement employers to reduce evidence of
a worker's employment, an amendment to the Wage Protection
Law put into effect in 2009 did try to challenge this by stating
that the burden of proof regarding attendance records falls on the
employer and if nothing could be provided, the court would *have*
to accept the attendance records of the worker.[6] Employers, however, continue the practice knowing that the obstacles in place for
workers in the first place (legal fees, work permit records, records
of work hours and payment, signed contract agreement as well as
the possibility of being blacklisted) will prevent the vast majority
from getting their day in court. Although many employers simply reacted to the amendment by recording false information on
the records they keep or claiming fewer work days than workers
had actually carried out, so that they can then record on the pay
slip that the worker was being paid minimum wage when they
were not (Kav LaOved, 2012: 33). It is the job of the middleman,

to not just hire and fire workers, but to make the whole process as ambiguous as possible.

This buffer is so effective that many workers don't even know the name of their Israeli employer. In some cases, workers' permits have included the middleman's name under the 'employer' title rather than their actual Israeli boss (Ibid: 41). A tactic that again allows the employer to ignore any queries or demands from workers regarding illegal work conditions and rights, instead pushing those problems on to the middleman, who, playing the enforcer role, will tell a worker to be quiet or risk their job and income.[7] It's a clever exploitative system that has been thought out and tinkered with extensively over the years. Middlemen are aggressive, motivated by money and have no problem in exploiting their own countrymen – over a fifth of Palestinian settlement workers have said they've been abused by them in the past (Sbeih, 2011).

Abed began working in the settlements two decades ago, first as a construction worker, but by using his working knowledge of Hebrew he begun to introduce himself to wealthy settlers and business owners who he thought might be looking for building work to get done. After a few rejections, one said yes. Abed said he had good connections, authority, and could get the men together easily, for a cheap price, and start straight away – he's not looked back since. Now employers approach him when they need workers. What workers under his command are paid varies he says, although 100–150 NIS is the general going rate for all forms of work – dangerous, safe, skilled, or unskilled. But Abed denies the charge of exploitation when he's asked if he believes the role he plays in the settlement work industry exploits the workers under his command. "There are so many people that want jobs, I help them get them. You know the people in the settlements they don't do these jobs [blue-collar work], they want Palestinians to do it for them," he says in his defence. "I look after them and pay well. But yes there are people [middlemen that exploit workers] like this. People are not angels."

"Israel is controlling the economy, controlling the products, they control everything, so we cannot develop ourselves, we're not being allowed to. If we had independence, our own state without occupation, then we could develop it, build it, and develop the economy. But right now, we can't do it, it is impossible."

Although he's right, Abed is part of that structure of control, something he will reluctantly admit. He supplies workers, and is paid well for the job, although he refuses to disclose how much. The workers he employs on the other hand and who work beside him get sometimes just half the legal minimum wage for a day's work. While Abed says he gets a set rate per day and per worker he provides, other middlemen may take their wage directly from what employers set aside to pay workers – it's a clever system. Employers scout out a middleman to find workers, the deal being that the middleman will be paid from taking money from the workers' salaries, which are set at the lowest allowed legally, 25 NIS an hour. The company looks legitimate on paper, providing pay slips to Israeli authorities that show legal amounts being paid, yet workers are getting far less than the paperwork reveals. A middleman will then, after discussion with the employer around the exact figure, skim for example 5 or 10 NIS from each worker's wage per hour to create their own wage. The middleman's wage is left absent from documentation, and the worker's wage looks legal, yet while the latter is grossly underpaid, the former takes home a big paycheck. The employer's business looks above board.

Middlemen may not even apply for permits for workers. Qassem,[8] a middleman from Nahalin, explained that he purposefully used workers who could not get permits or were blacklisted, because the companies he works with preferred illegal workers which they can then pay less, make them work longer hours, and who they do not need to register. "If I need another five workers tomorrow, it will be so easy to find them," Qassem says when asked how easy it would be to get more workers quickly if an employer asked him. "All of the people in the West Bank who are not working, and there are many, are waiting for work."

Keeping a good relationship with middlemen has become a must for Palestinian workers. Yet rightly, many see them as a direct part of the Israeli occupation, helping to exploit the Palestinian workforce for their own financial benefit. They earn well, and not just through their own wage, but also through backchannel means. Legal settlement employment requires a permit, and middlemen have the ability to grant workers those permits. They hold power in that respect over a group desperate for an income and who depend on them financially. This allows them to wield power over workers as well as give them the ability to grant preferential treatment to those that curry favour. They are certainly not equal opportunity employers. Permits are rarely supplied free of charge and corruption is rife. Middlemen often charge either a one-off fee for a permit, or charge a monthly one for providing and renewing the documentation.[9] These fees and other expenses can dig substantially into an already low wage. Working long hours, for five or six days a week, a worker may bring home anything between 2,000 to 3,500 NIS a month for his family, and that's without the price of a permit, transport, or any other fees siphoned out.[10] In the agricultural settlements in the Jordan

Valley where wages for Palestinian farm workers are at a far lower rate than other settlement work, the wages can be far less than that.[11] And the permits may not even be real. A black market has cropped up where some middlemen have started producing fake permits by simply copying the blueprint of real ones and swapping names. Workers desperate for employment go looking for middlemen to provide them with permits, but some of them are given fake ones and are told that the documents are real and Israeli government issued and approved. Mousa,[12] a talented chef in his late twenties, knows the potential problems of these fake permits well. He says he paid 2,000 NIS straight up for a permit he believed was real from a middleman he knew personally. That 2,000 NIS cost him 21 days in jail. An Israeli soldier checked the permit against stored records at a checkpoint just a matter of days after he first received it. The permit was fake.

"I spent twenty-one days in jail because of a false permit. And twenty-one days was excellent," Mousa says jokingly with the sort of dark humour that is found up and down the West Bank in the face of Israeli occupation. "It could have been much longer, they put people in jail for months, years. But they knew I had no idea it was fake. If they thought I knew it was illegal, I'm sure I would have spent six months in jail." Mousa was lucky, he knows other workers that haven't been.

"I consider myself a criminal," Abed says with remarkable honesty after talking for some time. He claims he has never provided a fake permit and never will, though admits the practice exists. His criminality, he says, is being complicit in the creation and continuation of the illegal Israeli settlements. "I'm building on Palestinian land. If it's on pre-67' lands [Inside the 1949 Armistice Line/Green Line], then for me it is fine it is ok, but in the settlements, then no, it's not good. Look at the building developments here in the West Bank, you have to ask permission to build almost everywhere, permission from the Israelis, and they almost always say no. Why? Because they want to keep us building in the settlements, and doing it cheap for them, than us building for Palestinians and our country."

THREE | Underpaid and underage, the child workers of the valley

"Really, there are children working everywhere here. All around us," Hamza Zubeidat, the highly driven NGO worker and Jordan Valley activist says as he drives down the Jordan Valley's Highway 90. Pristine Israeli settlements and their adjoining lush green farms, large greenhouses, and polytunnels flank the road. As Hamza takes the car past a farm adjoined to the settlement of Yafit, three young teenagers can be seen sitting on a small bank of dirt. It's midday, the sun is beating down, and they look exhausted. On other farms lining the valley the same exhausted expressions appear again and again amongst the rows of crops. Palestinian adults and children picking vegetables, digging holes and trenches, tending to Palestinian land now annexed by settlements and owned by Israeli farmers. It can be backbreaking work and for very little money, in temperatures that can often reach over 40 degrees Celsius in the summer. Agricultural work is not just incredibly tiring; it's also one of the worst paid employment sectors for Palestinian settlement workers. With Thai migrant workers making up 95 percent of the agricultural workforce in Israel and the settlements, and being subjected themselves routinely to labour abuses and less than minimum wage (Vickery, 2016a) – albeit not to the same extent as Palestinian settlement workers – the wage for Palestinians working in the farms has plummeted due to the availability of another cheap workforce that are tied to the agricultural sector through a bilateral agreement between Israel and Thailand. Palestinians here not only feel forced to work in the settlements, they have to do so for wages that can be as little as 50 or 60 NIS a day.

Hamza, a Palestinian Bedouin from Az-Zubeidat village in the valley has been raising the issue of child labour in the settlements for years with his work for Palestinian NGO MA'AN Development Center. He works at a million miles an hour, taking phone calls and doing radio interviews to stations in Palestine and Jordan. Injustice in the Jordan Valley, and the exploitation of the people here, is a cause close to his heart. Hamza's own mother works in the settlements picking herbs for 70 NIS a day. Children from his hometown, as well as surrounding areas such as Fasayll and Al-Jiflik, are dropping out of school as early as the age of 11 to help bring in money for their penniless families. Settlement farms seem only to keen to employ them.

Passing the red tiled roofs and concreted roads of Tomer settlement, Hamza takes a quick left down a dirt road towards Fasayll, a Palestinian village of 1,200 set against a background of rolling hills marking the edge of the valley. The backdrop is beautiful, but forbidden. The dusty land that encircles the village doesn't appear to be in use, but it still comes under the control of the Israeli settlement and ever present military. The cramped village and the road leading in and out are the only places residents are allowed to go freely.

Fasayll couldn't be more different from its well-to-do neighbour. The small grey concrete modest homes, some with just corrugated tin for a roof, are cramped, housing large families. Children wander the dirt roads and paths of the village in broken sandals and worn-down clothes. Disposable income isn't a concept here.

In a small one-roomed concrete structure near the entrance of the village, 15-year-old Yazan[1] is waiting. The shy teenager has just finished work for the day and is wary to speak at first – friends of his have been fired for speaking out about their work in the past. He may hate the hard farm work, but being dismissed would be catastrophic for his family.

"If I'm honest, I feel shame from this work," he confides, talking about his employment in a settlement farm in neighbouring Tomer. "I have to work there, the money situation is not good." Without the money he makes – a meager 70 NIS a day for 8 hour's work, less than 10 NIS an hour – Yazan says his family can't afford their expenses. It's a tiring existence.

Yazan's family barely scrape a living already. Working the farms in the settlements of Tomer, Pez'al, and Yafit that surround the village, along with doing what sheep and goat farming they can – the family's traditional form of income – just about gets them by. Like almost all Palestinian families here in the valley though, that traditional form of income is fast disappearing, if not gone already for most. Settlement work has become the main employment sector. Area C, which encompasses 90 percent of the Jordan Valley, is mostly a no-go zone for Palestinians. Concrete blocks with the words *Firing Zone* scribbled on them in Arabic, Hebrew, and English dot the valley – closed military zones that have annexed nearly half of the land here, and much of the grazing land that Palestinian farmers and herders used to rely on. Twenty-six Israeli state-designated nature reserves take up another 20 percent of the land – land forbidden for farming, grazing, and herding. Minefields that still scatter the area from the 1948 Arab-Israeli War make up another 1 percent. The 39 Israeli settlements and the large swathes of land that come under their control, take up much of the remaining land. In reality they work similarly to the closed military zones albeit with one glaring difference – set foot on settlement land and expect trouble, unless of course it's a workday and you're employed by a settler. In total for the Palestinians that live here, 85.2 percent of the land in the Jordan Valley is off-limits. Areas where they are not allowed to farm, herd, cultivate, build, and in many cases even walk on.

For families who want to carry on the traditional herding and farming lifestyle, they must stump up the money to rent land, often their own stolen land from Israeli authorities and settlers, or keep animals within the close confines of the village boundaries and buy expensive feed for them. It's an option very few are able to afford. In reality, the animals and the people have the same restrictions on movement, a fact that is not lost on shepherds around the valley.

Yazan, 15 years old, knows the problems of growing up and living here all too well. "I don't have a choice but to work there," he says of the settlements, gaining in confidence as he speaks. "And I know they should pay us more, I know it is not the law. I tried to ask for more, but the settler refused. He just answered no and said, 'This is what I give to you, if you like it take it, if you don't, then leave.' What choice do I have?"

The teenager talks as though he expects trouble for admitting that he works on a settlement farm, "I don't feel good working there," he repeats again looking for a level of understanding for his situation from the people around him. There's no judgment in the village though, settlement work is by far the biggest employment sector.

Yazan was first employed at the age of 14, working five days a week, eight hours a day, picking sweet peppers and boxing them. He spends his days toiling the farm, carrying large boxes, and bending over to pick from the ground in tiring and often grueling weather conditions – in the polytunnels during summer, the temperature often reaches 50 degrees Celsius. He already has back pain, and longs to stop working at the farm, but he can't see an end to it. Still, he says he dreams of being a policeman. A job where he could enforce the law – a job he wishes someone would do with his boss.

"You know, sometimes the settlers come and they just start screaming at us about the work. Sometimes he [settler employer] fires people just to show how angry he is. They are always screaming bad stuff, I can't say what. They are cursing all the time, and because we are Muslims, the farmer is always cursing my religion."

Yazan's situation is not unique. Hundreds of children work in the settlements in the valley, some as young as 11 (Human Rights Watch, 2015). Israeli law stipulates that employment of any child 14 or under is prohibited.[2] A child aged 15 can be employed as long as the work won't harm the child's health and wellbeing. The tiring agricultural work, however, can cause multiple health problems especially for a child that is still growing. It involves the use of heavy machinery and hazardous pesticides, and all without proper safety equipment and training. The use of pesticides in this way allows for easy absorption into the respiratory system and the skin, causing skin problems, allergies, dizziness, lack of appetite, and for children who are still developing and more sensitive to the chemicals than their adult colleagues, there is a danger of developing cancer and infertility (Kav LaOved, 2009a).

Injuries, and a lack of care for workers' safety are common in the settlement farms. Workers on date farms frequently suffer infections from scratches and injuries from date palm thorns while working without gloves. One set of workers at a date farm were even reported to have been lifted by a crane and forced to climb into the trees – all without safety gear or equipment – where they were then left for several hours ordered by their employer to harvest dates while clinging to the branches. They were allowed no breaks, and were forced to relieve themselves while in the trees, rather than being allowed down (Kav LaOved, 2009b). There have also been several accidents where serious injuries and fatalities have been recorded from the collapse of unsafe cranes during harvest season (Kav LaOved, 2012: 48). Agricultural work in the settlements is not just backbreaking, it's dangerous.

"If they [the settlers] were not here, we would be allowed on the land," Yazan says when asked what life would be like without the settlements. "Own the land and cultivate it, and make an actual income. We could live."

There is a mix of anger and upset in the teenager's voice. His face is one of despondence. Yazan may be young, but his words echo loudly around the Palestinian communities of the valley. The overwhelming feeling is that while Palestinian families have suffered, Israeli settlers have benefitted. And not just through land. But also through gaining a cheap labour source from an impoverished Palestinian population with high unemployment levels and very few income options. The stifling reality of the occupation in the valley has not just led adults to work in the settlements, but has seen their children following behind them in tow. Their childhoods lost in settlement farms amongst the rows of vegetables they must dig, and the date palms they must harvest.

"They don't care about our salaries, do you think they will care about our age?" Yazan asks, though he doesn't seem to be looking for an answer. "It's not about rights. It's just because we're Palestinian."

"It's all about profit in the end," Hamza quips. "What he [the farmer] does care about, is the numbers at the end of the day."

Workers' rights don't rule in the valley, money does. It's a recurring theme in settlement work throughout the occupied West Bank.

Sitting opposite Yazan in the small one-roomed building – which seems pretty standard for the village – Abu Fuad[3] the *Mukhtar* [council leader] of Fasayll nods in agreement. "We're not treated like equals here, animals are treated better. For them [settlers], we are a way to make money, that's it. Our sons and our family members work in the settlements because our only income came from animal farming, but we can't use the land now."

Abu Fuad, a highly respected figure in Fasayll, begins to list incidents that have happened to villagers when they've tried to go against Israeli military rule and use the surrounding land for livestock. One of the settlers shot a shepherd last year he says, and two of his family members have been arrested for trying to use grazing land in military zones. Another villager had his sheep taken by the army. These and other incidents have made villagers scared to leave Fasayll. There is one exception however. The road leading out of the village to the highway and to the settlement farms never has any problems.

Abu Fuad sighs as he speaks, "This year it is so green," he says talking of the hills around the village that would make for perfect grazing land. "But we can't go to the mountains, we can't go to other areas as it's beside the settlements. This is their strategy, to force the people to work in the settlements."

He remembers a time when it was easier to live in the valley. Before the occupation of the West Bank, livestock and shepherds could roam more freely. With occupation in 1967 times were difficult, but there were still some possibilities. As the years have gone on however, more land was taken, more settlements appeared, and with their creation and expansion, the land and traditional livelihood was lost. The Palestinian population in the valley has subsequently decreased from an estimated 250,000 in 1967, to around 60,000 five decades later, as the harsh realities of occupation have forced residents out of the area in order to find a livelihood and to survive.[4]

The expansion, of both the settlements and their large agricultural projects, doesn't look like it will end anytime soon. Both also have no problem with water supply, a constant problem for Palestinian families. The World Health Organization recommends a minimum of 100 litres per person per day. Israeli settlers however have a domestic consumption of three times that. That number for Palestinians on the other hand, is just 73. For Palestinian families not connected to the water grid and who rely solely on water trucks and rainwater, that fluctuates down to between 20–50 litres (Carton, 2015). All settlement communities are connected to the water network, yet more than 70 percent of Palestinian communities in Area C are not (OCHA, 2014a). The problem of water, or more so lack of it in the region in general, has been cited as the main reason why the Israeli government has ensured such a tight grip on the land of the valley – which contains large underground water reservoirs – and in the future will continue to do so (Stork, 1983; Wolf, 1995). For now, although water reservoirs exist under the ground, only one working well remains in Palestinian hands in the valley. The rest of the water is controlled by the Israeli government and military – and it's clear where it is going. When water supply is low in summer, the Israeli national water company that supplies Palestinians with water, Mekorot, has been known to shut off supply to Palestinian towns and villages in order to ensure a constant supply for settlements (Ma'an, 2015). Walking around the Israeli settlements with the greenery on show and their well-irrigated farms, it's clear to see that water isn't a problem for everyone in the valley.

The valley itself has vast agricultural potential, yet the lack of access for Palestinians to cultivate it, along with the issue of water not being freely available for them, has turned the Jordan Valley and Jericho area into the least cultivated Palestinian area in the West Bank. One collection of Israeli and Palestinian economists believe that if the growing technologies that have been honed in the cramped confines of the Gaza Strip were applied to 100,000 dunums (10,000 hectares) in the Jordan Valley, the resulting agricultural production would provide a staggering 150,000–200,000 new direct and indirect jobs (Arnon and Bamya, 2010: 239). Such a move would transform the valley, boost the Palestinian economy, and provide tens of thousands of jobs to Palestinians in the area. But this would require Israel relinquishing control of large parts of rich farmland in the valley to Palestinian control – a move no-one expects to happen anytime soon, least of all Abu Fuad. "They won't allow us to farm, if we do, then we don't need to work for them [Israeli settlers] for cheap, and our farms will then compete directly against them. They will never let this happen."

"What can we do?" he asks a few minutes later. "If money coming from sheep farming is not enough, and we can't farm ourselves, then it's not just the adults here that have to work, the kids stop school and go to work too. They pay us so little."

It's clear the idea doesn't sit well with him. He's the leader of a Palestinian village where both adults and children scrape a living doing cheap labour for the same people that now live on the land that the people of Fasayll used to work on for themselves. There is no pride in the work, enjoyment, or sense of worth. It's merely a way to live.

"There's no money in school"

"There are younger children than me working on the farm," Yazan says when asked about the people he works with. "About twenty are younger, many are my age."

Mohammed,[5] a 14-year-old from the village is one of those younger workers. Mohammed who is autistic, struggles with simple questions, often gets confused, and has problems with motor coordination, yet he works between 8–10 hours a day, four days a week, shoveling dirt and digging holes on a settlement farm. He has an infectious smile, and surprisingly seems full of energy having just spent several hours working on the farm. His face lights up when he begins talking about his father – his favourite topic of conversation. The smile soon leaves Mohammed when he's asked about his employer.

"He shouts, he comes sometimes just to shout at the work I'm doing," Mohammed says with the friendly face of Abu Fuad nearby giving him encouragement and confidence to speak. "Sometimes he fires workers. It scares me." Mohammed's sandals are ripped and torn, and his feet are still coated in mud from the day's work. It's not an easy life for the kid. "Going to school would be easier," the 14-year-old says when asked about what he

would do rather than work. "But there's no money in school."
There is however, money in settlement work – though not much.
Mohammed earns just 60 NIS a day.

Public transport barely exists in the valley so travelling for work
elsewhere to the Palestinian cities is difficult and expensive. The
regular scheduled green Israeli buses that serve the highway that
splits the valley in half are for Israeli citizens only. In many ways,
Israelis can travel around parts of the West Bank, and certainly
the valley, more easily than Palestinians can.

Mohammed doesn't have far to travel. A 20 minute walk at
5am takes him to the entrance of the settlement farm, from there a
tractor picks him up and delivers him to the spot where he must
work. The junctions where the main highway meets the roads into
the settlements are hives of activity in the morning, with Palestinian workers, many of them children, congregating before work.
All up before sunrise and into the farms early – being late risks
being fired on the spot. Easy for employers to do, when there
are hundreds more Palestinians needing jobs in the impoverished
Palestinian areas, waiting for the call from a Palestinian middleman to begin work.

Laith,[6] who is just 12, works for a settler planting crops though
a Palestinian middleman he knows as Abu Youssef. He's been
working for six months for two or three days a week, although
unlike Mohammed and Yazan, he still manages to attend some
school classes. He expects to completely drop out soon.

"I need to give some money to my family," he says when asked
why he works. Laith is lively and full of confidence when he talks.
Like most Palestinian children, he's highly politically aware – it
comes with the reality of living under occupation and having your
life dictated from above by Israel so obviously.

"Of course it would be better without the occupation here," he says loudly and with conviction. "Then we could work for ourselves, maybe I would not need to work at all. I know around thirty children who are working, if it was different maybe everyone could all be in school."

Laith seems several years his senior when he speaks. His childhood has been warped with worries around possible Israeli army incursions into his village to demolish homes or make arrests, along with the knowledge that, economically, things have and will remain a struggle. It takes a while for him to start speaking about topics other than the occupation or work. Eventually be begins to talk about his hobbies – he's a keen footballer and Barcelona FC fan – and like Yazan, he wishes to train as a policeman. But he doesn't allow himself long to flirt with the idea of a better future. "But there's no money. This is why we work."

"The settler doesn't care"

"They are forcing us, because of the situation, to have our kids leave the school early," Jamela,[7] a kind-hearted women in her early 50s, explains from Az-Zubeidat village a few miles up the valley and north of Fasayll. The village's dusty streets have dozens of young children under the age of ten playing with whatever they can get their hands on. Groups of kids run up and down the roads chasing each other, one young boy plays with a discarded hubcap which he drags along the ground with enthusiasm using a piece of string attached to the metal. There is a distinct lack of children aged over ten.

"They're working in the settlements," Jamela says when questioned about the village's other children. Jamela works in a settlement farm herself, earning 60 NIS for between 8–10 hours picking herbs. It's a common job for Palestinian women in the valley. Women make up around a tenth of all Palestinian workers in the settlements, working almost exclusively in the agriculture and service sectors. They are subjected to a greater degree of exploitation by their employers with wages that are on average just half of what adult Palestinian male workers get on a daily basis (Sbeih, 2011). Jamela earns around 7 NIS an hour, but for female Palestinian settlement workers, this is the norm.

Jamela's children work in the settlements too. She desperately wishes they didn't have to. Behind her on the wall of her home, a colourful Bedouin farming scene has been painted out. Shepherds and sheep all going about their daily business in the valley. It's a scene from Jamela's childhood, before the occupation.

"We don't have this life anymore," she says gesturing towards the mural behind her. "Look at the settlers, look at their kids. Their kids can go to school, get an education, they can become engineers, pilots. Not like our children."

Away from Jamela's home, half a dozen Israeli army jeeps rumble slowly by on the nearby Highway 90. Following them, an armoured Caterpillar trudges behind – it's a convoy that brings fear into the heart of Palestinian communities here. Home demolitions are a daily occurrence in the valley, where it is virtually impossible to get any form of building work authorised by Israel.[8] Further down the highway, in an area safe from the military jeeps, for today at least, 14-year-old Zacharia[9] and 16-year-old Mohammed[10] wait at the side of the road near Tomer and Gilgal settlements as their day's work comes to an end. Zacharia gives an enthusiastic *ahlan-wa-sahlan* (welcome in Arabic), but looks exhausted. It's hot, the sun is beating down, and both have been working the fields since 6am in the morning. They're lucky if they manage to get a thirty-minute break from picking peppers and onions all day, they say. Moving away from the busy highway, and settling under the welcoming shade of a nearby tree amongst the green Khubeza plant – a native vegetation of the valley that is used by poorer families for cooking – Zacharia begins to talk about his work.

"Last month the tractor drove over my foot," he says wincing and gesturing towards his left leg as he sits on the ground. "My father had to take me to hospital, the farmer didn't care. He just told me I can phone my father and he can take me there. I just had to sit there and wait in pain for half an hour. My family had to pay for all the hospital fees."

Zacharia's foot was broken from the incident. The farmer gave him 70 NIS a day for two weeks while he was recovering. The same amount he receives for a day's shift working on the farm – 15 NIS less an hour than the legal minimum wage. Like almost all Palestinian workers in the settlement farms, the teenager says health insurance wasn't part of his contract, or an option. The only contract he received, along with 16-year-old Mohammed who works for the same employer, was a piece of paper he was given at the start of his employment – when he was just 13 – stating that he agreed that he wasn't allowed to claim compensation if he was sacked or for injuries obtained during work. He wasn't allowed to begin work without signing the document.

"The settler doesn't care," he says. "We have no rights, no insurance. To be honest, the work affects me, it's hard, I don't like it, it makes me depressed. But I have nothing else, it's the only place I can work, and my family need me to help out."

When asked whether he knew that the minimum wage was 25 NIS an hour, and that the farmer by law had to pay that, Zacharia looks surprised. His eyes light up briefly at the idea of earning so much for an hour's work before he glances towards the ground. "I feel used by the farm," he says quietly.

"It wouldn't matter if we knew this before or not," Mohammed says joining the conversation. "He [the farmer] has said before that if one of us takes him to court for anything, then he will fire us all. He has threatened us all with this. We can't complain about anything, or ask for better conditions or money, because we will make a problem for everyone working."

It's not an uncommon threat. Palestinian workers are frequently punished for attempts at forming unions and lobbying for their rights (see Chapter 5).

For both Mohammed and Zacharia, working in the settlements is an unfortunate family affair. Their siblings and parents work in the settlements also, picking and packaging vegetables and dates.

"There are no other job opportunities for us here," Zacharia says with a palpable sadness in his voice. During harvest season the two teenagers say they have to work from 8am until 8pm. For the 12-hour stint,[11] they receive the same 10 NIS an hour wage. If they tell the farmer they don't want to work the extra hours, they say they will be fired.

"They don't have the right to say they are doing something good for us by employing us," the younger teenager says when asked about what he would say if the farmer claimed they were doing a good thing by employing Palestinians – rhetoric that is often espoused by Israeli politicians when questioned about the use of Palestinian labour in the settlements. "We don't have any choice but to take their jobs. They know this, so they know they can treat us badly."

"We have to go," Mohammed says suddenly as cars continue to rumble past nearby. Both are nervous to be caught speaking about their work, they always have the looming possibility of dismissal hanging over their head. The idea of losing their jobs and putting their families in financial jeopardy is a terrifying one for both.

"You see the children working here," Hamza says after the children swiftly leave. "It can't be denied. But ask any settler farmer and they will deny that they are employing children in the farms."

Hamza's not wrong. "There is nothing like this," Shaul,[12] an Israeli farmer in Tomer settlement remarks defensively when questioned about child labour in the Jordan Valley settlements. "I don't know it and I don't know anyone that does it. Palestinians will always complain."

FOUR | Occupation's ultimate humiliation

"They are enjoying their lives"

"Please, let's do this quickly," Hamza pleads, saying the words quickly and quietly. "Because for them to be honest, this is embarrassing."

It's a warm spring day back in Az-Zubeidat, Hamza's hometown. The two elderly women sitting opposite us on a beaten-up old sofa have warm welcoming smiles, but they take their time to open up. The topic isn't an easy one for them. Rather, it is one that fills them with shame. They not only work on the settlement farms that flank the village, but the land that those farms now sit on was previously owned and cultivated by the women's families before it was annexed for Israel's settlement project in the valley.

It's not just a case of working in the settlements; it's one of working on your own stolen land for the profit of the people who benefitted from that annexation and your family's loss.

"My family used to farm that land. But they [Israel] stole it," Faiza[1] says. "Our only way to have work now is to work under them. They [the settlers] are very happy, they have money. They are enjoying their lives."

Faiza, an elderly woman in her sixties, works like many Palestinian women in the poverty-stricken villages of the Jordan Valley picking and packaging herbs in the settlement farms. Her

husband, she says, after decades of tilling the ground in the settlements, is now too sick to work. She is the main breadwinner for
the family but earns just 60–70 NIS a day. She frequently gets
ill from the pesticides used, and throws up at least once a week
while at work because of them. Her coarse and scarred hands,
now shaky with decades of hard labour and age, cause her problems as she works. She often painfully slices herself with knives
by accident as she's cutting and bundling the herbs. She just has
to patch up the wounds herself with spare pieces of cloth lying
around and get on with the work.

Faiza has fond memories of her childhood here. Life wasn't
easy growing up, but her family had the building blocks for a
decent life at their disposal. They had some land that they were
able to farm on, as well as a modest number of grazing animals.
They were not rich, and they assumed they never would be, but
it was enough. Faiza remembers playing in the land surrounding
the village, running after friends, and picking the springtime flow-
ers that create a colourful and attractive tapestry which coats the
hills of the valley as the mild winter ends and spring begins. She
talks with a melancholic nostalgia; it's clear she's thinking back
to those times in her head as she speaks, but it remains obvious
that she can never wrestle her current reality from her thoughts.
"I dream of going for a picnic in the hills now," she says, her eyes
seemingly focused somewhere in the distant past. She knows her
children didn't have the same childhood. The occupation brought
an end to freedom of movement in the valley, as land started to be
lost to military zones, settlements, or Israeli-state classified nature
reserves. Now with armed soldiers and settlers, and 90 percent
of the valley designated as Area C, venturing outside the village
isn't a potential adventure for children anymore – it's potentially

dangerous. The land became the settlers', as did the profit reaped from that land. And the ground Faiza played on, laughed on, and helped her family farm vegetables on, became, with Israeli occupation, a place in her adult life where she would work to scrape a living for herself, and bolster profit for her employers through her cheap labour, for the very occupiers who were granted the land of her childhood.

"Now we are working for them for very cheap," Faiza says sighing. "Sometimes just 50 NIS a day. If you're Israeli and you work you can make minimum 220 NIS.[2] 50 NIS is not even enough for dinner for the family at the end of the day. What can we do? We used to cultivate our own land, but now we can't. They control the land and the water. There is no water for us to use. You know, we are forced to do this work. We are doing it just to stay alive. We are not doing this because we want to or because we are making a lot of money."

"She's right," Fuzaylah,[3] sitting beside her says, joining the conversation. Fuzaylah another resident of Az-Zubeidat is in the same position as Faiza; she works on a farm attached to the settlement of Argaman – land that used to be cultivated by her parents.

"We are being used for profit, it's as simple as that," she says angrily. Fuzaylah doesn't seem concerned for talking or reminiscing about the past. She is angry at the occupation and happy to show it, but she's also angry at the situation it has forced her into, working on her family's own stolen land just to be able to put food on the table. "We don't have our land to do our own business, so we can't make anything for ourselves. They [Israel] know they can exploit us. We are opposed to this work, we have no opportunity, no other choice, there is nothing else for us. Israel, by occupying, have created a cheap workforce out of us, they know it and so do we."

Fuzaylah and Faiza aren't unique. Approximately 11 percent of Palestinian settlement workers are working on land that was owned by their immediate family or relatives (Sbeih, 2011). For people like Fuzaylah, to feel forced to work on land stolen from her family, and all to make profit for her occupiers, is the ultimate humiliation of occupation.

"It fills me with shame"

"I'm working on my own land, can you believe this is our situation?" Aymad,[4] an electrician, asks incredulously as he sits at a breakfast spot near his village of Nahalin.

"We, many of us, are working on land that has been stolen from our own families, from our own villages. Land that has been taken by the settlements or by the Wall. It fills me with shame."

Shame is a recurring theme for Palestinian workers, even more so for those working on the stolen land of their relatives. Aymad, a young man in his early 20s, has worked in several of the settlements that surround his hometown, including the large Beitar Illit settlement, a settlement that annexed much of his family's land.

"Working on land that I know was stolen from my family, but also land that I know was stolen from families I know – it feels terrible," he admits.

On most workdays, Aymad knows the Palestinian family whose land he is working and building the settlement infrastructure on. That family probably knows he's working on their annexed land as well, Aymad confesses, and it doesn't always sit well with them. Settlement work doesn't only bring shame to Palestinian workers, it also creates much animosity towards them.

Building the settlements, brick by brick

The wonky door of the small shop – which resembles a large animal shack more than anything else – is plastered with United Nations' food voucher posters. Items are listed in neat order, food that can be exchanged for the UNRWA tokens that are given out to struggling families.[5] Eggs, salt, chicken, butter, and assorted vegetables mainly. The basics. Another poster indicates how many of each item can be exchanged, depending on how big a family is and therefore how many mouths there are to feed. The vouchers are a lifeline for some families and without them they would go hungry. They also give as good an indication as any of how employment and consequently money is not easy to find here.

The shop is perched at the top of Al-Walaja, the village that seems to coherently sum up the depressing reality of Palestinian settlement work. It's got the Wall, it used to have land, it's a village of refugees who tried to recreate their arable lifestyle after displacement, but then along came the occupation in 1967, and the settlements and the Wall slowly took that land from them again. And now, down every street, and on every corner, there's a settlement worker, and opinions, both good and bad, about them.

Hakim[6] didn't want to meet on the street or in his home; not all of his relatives know he builds the settlements. The small one-roomed shop at the top of the village – owned by a good friend, and outside of the village center – was a place he said he would feel comfortable talking. Getting Hakim to this point was hard enough, the idea of speaking about his work to anyone filled him with dread, never mind the constant shame. It was his friend that convinced him to meet, explaining that it was an opportunity to explain *why* he worked in the building of the settlements. It wasn't an opportunity Hakim got often. When people found out about his building work in the past, he had been shouted at, called an Israeli spy and the conversation would end at that. There was never the opportunity to explain that he felt forced into it in order just to survive.

"I feel guilty about this work, people look to me like I am helping Israel," 23-year-old Hakim says, speaking quietly and looking down at the ground. "But really I feel I have no choice. If I could get a salary here [PA areas] I would stop working there immediately."

Much of Hakim's family land was taken with the onset of occupation. With the construction of the Wall beginning in 2002, five more dunums (half a hectare) were annexed. It wasn't enough land to make a living off, but that five dunums was enough to feed the family. When Hakim reached his late teens he began desperately searching for employment in order to help his family out. Eventually he approached a middleman who got him involved in construction jobs in the settlements. Now, he gets up at 4:30am in order to be at the settlement checkpoint at Beitar Illit for 5:30am where he stands rain or shine, hot or cold, until he's let though. Sometimes the Israeli soldiers make the process quick, sometimes Hakim says, they appear to be trying to be as slow as possible. If he's on the construction site any later than 7am, he will be fired. If he's ill, he still has to come into work in order to keep his job.

"But they sometimes just give me half a day's wage (75 NIS) instead of the full day's wage (150 NIS) if they know I am ill," he says.

"I know I don't get paid minimum wage. I feel the work I do deserves more than what I am paid. There are Israelis that work with me, that seem to do the same job but less work than me, who

work less hard, and get paid more than me, about 250 NIS a day."
On the rare occasions where Israeli citizens are working the same
blue-collar jobs as Palestinians in the settlements (see Chapter 6
regarding the segmentation of the Israeli labour market and blue-
collar work) they are granted their work and wage rights with no
problems, as enshrined in law, unlike their Palestinian counterparts. Israeli settlement workers earn double what Palestinian
settlement workers do (Bank of Israel, 2014). In most cases where
factories or businesses employ both Israeli and Palestinian workers however, the Israeli workers almost always occupy the non-
manual work, such as administrative jobs (Kav LaOved, 2013).

Unlike other settlement employment such as working in a
supermarket, construction jobs often ebb and flow depending on
the Israeli government's decisions regarding the expansion of the
settlements. This reality doesn't go unnoticed by construction
workers who are always walking an economic tightrope to survive. They know that if the government announces the creation
of new housing units at a particular settlement, then they should
have an opportunity to gain employment in the near future and
subsequently an income stream with which to look after their
family. But they also know that such an announcement means
the physical expansion of the settlements, and on one level has
the potential to take more Palestinian land and ruin livelihoods,
and on another is illegal, against international law, is protested
by the Palestinian Authority government, Palestinian society and
the wider BDS movement and increases Israeli control, militar-
ily, as well as politically in regards to any peace deal made in the
future regarding land swaps. Construction workers breathe a sigh
of relief that they have work, but know their people and country
are going to be affected negatively from it.

Hakim says he feels guilty about the work he does, believing it to be, in his opinion, the worst form of settlement employment in regards to the ending of the occupation and Palestinian self-determination, "but all settlement work is in the same river," he says unconvincingly, as though trying to comfort himself about his specific settlement building role.

"I know that people outside don't see the full picture, they might think that the settlements are good for us as they provide work, but really there is no choice for us but to work there. To build them. We [settlement workers] feel abandoned."

Construction workers like Hakim, make up around half of all Palestinians employed in the Israeli labour market, yet job security for them is low, they can be fired or hired at a whim, while worksite conditions are dangerous. Accidents are frequent, increasing every year in the construction sector (Kav LaOved, 2016). With little to no government enforcement of safety regulations, or workers' rights for Palestinians in the settlements, employers have no incentive to improve the already hazardous and potentially fatal work environments that already exist.[7] Falling from height while working on buildings – often without proper safety equipment, training, and supervision – is the most common cause of injury (Ibid). Although Israeli labour law (which incorporates the settlements) stipulates that any incident must be documented, the worker sent immediately to an Israeli hospital, and compensation to be provided, this rarely happens. Injured workers are frequently sent to the underfunded and ill-prepared Palestinian hospitals in the West Bank, rather than specialist hospitals in Israel, allowing employers to avoid their financial responsibility to the law. Impoverished Palestinian families have to pick up the hospital bill in the aftermath and during rehabilitation periods, which can often be lengthy as workers recover from serious injuries. All workers should be insured by law, as their employer is responsible for making National Insurance payments for their employees. However with fake documentation, or no documentation or registration of workers rife, the process of gaining that compensation money is difficult. Employers will even avoid phoning for an ambulance so there is no record of any injury taking place at their premises – even if the worker has serious injuries.[8] Ahmad,[9] a construction worker who was working at a building site in the Mishor Adumim industrial zone fell six meters after a roof he was standing on caved in. He broke his back.

"My boss put me in his car and drove me from where the accident was to the entrance of the settlement," Ahmad says of the incident. "He just left me there and said, "Go and get treatment in your own [PA] area." I tried to move but I couldn't, eventually I managed to call my brother who came to the entrance and got me to hospital."

Cases like this in construction are not uncommon, and often result in workers getting no compensation or nowhere near what they are entitled to. In reality, the odds are heavily stacked in an employer's favour in any work accident dispute. An employer must sign off documents that state that the accident took place, yet unsurprisingly, considering the culture of exploitation in the settlements, many refuse to do so.[10] To get to that stage in the first place, workers must already be well-versed in their rights, obtain the relevant documents and know what to do with them. A rarity of sorts among Palestinian settlement workers where documents are often not translated into Arabic from Hebrew, who have no trade union (see Chapter 5), and where there is a culture of employers making absolutely no effort to alert workers to their rights in the first place. Many workers' do not even know that Israel has a minimum wage law that applies to them, never mind other rights and benefits they are legally entitled to.

Construction workers like Ahmad and Hakim don't have it easy. The job is hazardous, work is mainly temporary and relies heavily on government announcements regarding the building of new settlement housing units, and it's a highly shameful form of work vis-à-vis wider Palestinian society and their own self-determination aspirations. Like Hakim, many are unwilling to talk openly about their work and some try to keep it from their family and friends. Even workers' rights organisations can struggle at times to reach these workers, compared to other settlement workers, who are usually more willing to approach or be approached.

"Shame," Taghrid Shbita[11] a Palestinian fieldworker with Kav LaOved, an Israeli Workers' Rights Organisation, says to explain why there are difficulties in getting construction workers to come forward and document their working conditions, exploitation, and poor pay. "The employee has to serve and build on their own conquered land, employed under exploitative conditions, sometimes being addressed in humiliating ways, and yet he must surrender and be nice, be silent about the violations while employers suggest that there is no alternative [to current pay, working conditions]. Most individuals have no other source of income."

Settlement construction workers are a sensitive subject which everyone has an opinion on. Take one of the many *service* (8-seater shared Palestinian taxis) around the West Bank and ask the cross-section of passengers about their thoughts on them and they vary from some sympathy and understanding of the situation, although in the minority, to the more common view that the work is traitorous. Settlement work in general may be looked down on but understood by some as a necessity for families to survive where no other employment options exist. Construction work specifically, however, appears the exception to the rule and is seen as mainly inexcusable.[12]

"They are the same as an Israeli soldier," one man spat out when asked about his opinion on construction workers.[13] "If a settlement worker like this comes to me and starts speaking about the [PA] government or the president, and having an opinion, I tell them – you are like Israeli people, you are like a spy to us, you can't say anything."

In a place where settlements and occupation affect everyday life, everyone has an opinion on settlement work. The settlements after all continue to have a detrimental effect on Palestinian lives, and on a larger national scale, Palestinian aspirations for state-hood. "We feel angry that they do this," Hussain Foqha,[14] direc-tor of the PGFTU says when asked about the role of Palestinian construction workers. "They are devastating our land by build-ing the settlements, yet we are against the settlements, we fight against the settlements also. But this is the situation, it is unique here. There are 350,000 unemployed people, families need to live, they just want an opportunity, any opportunity to have a chance to live, we can't just make them stop, they are forced by their needs."

For construction workers, the feeling that there is no other choice appears even more prevalent than with other settlement workers. "Why else would I build their state and ruin mine, if I had a choice?" is the question asked, and it is hard to dis-agree. Workers feel complicit in the continuation and crucially, the expansion of, Israeli occupation in the West Bank, and the negative consequences of this for the Palestinian population. There is no reason they would do this willingly considering the shame from it, and the poor pay, but crucially, the negative and crushing impact the settlements continued existence and expansion has on their lives, their families' lives, and Palestinian lives in general. The work is also dangerous, the pay not more or less than any other settlement work (between 100–150 NIS a day) with the exception of agricultural work which is by far the lowest of all (60–80 NIS a day), and it affords them no respect in Palestinian society, and arguably, the lowest status of all settlement workers, a group that already occupies a particularly low status in Palestinian society anyway.

"But they [Israel] limit us, with what ways to go, with what we can do," Khalid, a construction worker who is currently unemployed and waiting for building work says explaining his difficulty in traveling across the West Bank in the hope of finding employment away from the settlements. When settlements expand, he gets work, when building is slow, he's often laid off. Money is always tight, and he saves what he can for the unemployed periods. Marrying or having a family is far from his mind. He barely manages to sustain himself. Travelling around to find work is not just an added expense he cannot afford, but may not even be possible. The road network in the West Bank has been created in such a way that cities and towns can be cut off from each other easily and quickly with makeshift Israeli military checkpoints that can close these arteries between major hubs, or drastically elongate travelling times as cars and their occupants go through lengthy checks and searches.[15] In times of escalation in the conflict, this not only happens frequently, but clashes and deaths of travelling Palestinians are not uncommon. Understandably, some

Palestinians choose not to take the risk and limit their movements. All is not conducive to holding down employment in a city tens of miles away, particularly in an occupied land where on a good day for example, travelling between Ramallah and Bethlehem, a distance of 14 miles as the crow flies, can still take two hours. On a bad day when soldiers have set up new checkpoints and are searching vehicles, that time can double or even triple. "If you want to go to one city, they give us only one way to get there, you don't have any other choice," Khalid says.

"You don't have a free choice. Even if you want to walk somewhere, you have to think, can I do this, should I go there. You have to think a lot about these things because it can be dangerous for you. But even for settlement work, they limit you, they control that too. When they need you, you go, when they don't they tell you to go away. One time a soldier said to me, "If we want to prevent Arabs from working we can do this, but now we want you to go and work." They make you work when they want, they control who, when, how many."

Khalid says that while he needs the work, he still fears it, and not because of the hazardous nature of the job, but rather the proliferation of guns and the power that soldiers and settlers can and do wield over Palestinian workers.

"When I go to the checkpoint to enter the settlement for work, the Israelis there treat us like animals. They force us to stand for hours waiting to go through. The soldiers point the guns at us like we are criminals. The settlers have done this also while we're working. To be honest, I am always afraid when working because of this. They hate Palestinian people, but they want us to work there so that we can build their houses for them cheaply, but when we are finished, then we are chucked out."

"I hate this work," he says with anger in his voice. "And I know there are people that have this idea that I am a traitor for it – and I understand it, I agree with it even, but I don't have another choice, I have to do this."

FIVE | The wretched of the Holy Land

A disposable workforce

Mohammed remembers the silence and darkness that night with chilling clarity. All in their 20s, Mohammed and his brothers had lived in their parent's home in the rural village of Sa'ir their whole life. Money had always, for as long as he could remember, been tight. And work had always been difficult to come by, even for the well-educated and determined Mohammed – called Hamouda by his friends and family. It was 3am, and he assumed he was the only person still awake in his little village nestled in the Hebron Hills in the southern West Bank. Hamouda should have been sleeping, but his mind was still racing. He had to get up in two hours for the tiring commute past Israeli soldiers and through checkpoints to his building work in a nearby Israeli settlement, but the empty bed of his brother, gunned down the day before after an alleged stabbing attack on the occupying Israeli soldiers nearby, haunted him.[1]

Hamouda wasn't alone for long. It had just passed three in the morning when a dozen fully armed Israeli soldiers burst into his home. His mother, father, younger brother and himself were rounded up. Half of the soldiers raided the house, overturning cabinets, and rooting through drawers clearly looking for something. The other soldiers stood, guns cocked towards the frightened family.

"They raided the whole place, and then one of them finally asked me if I had a permit from the settlement to work there. He demanded I give it to him. When I handed it over he tore it in half, set it on fire with a lighter, looked at me and said – 'now you have no work.'"[2] With his permit destroyed, the soldiers left, and Hamouda's income was gone.

Hamouda had just become a victim of Israel's policy of immediately revoking the permits of relatives of Palestinians killed in the on-going Israel/Palestine conflict. The reasoning according to the state, is that immediate family members of a Palestinian killed become a threat to Israel due to the potential for revenge attacks (Machsom Watch, 2007: 30–31). While the actual destruction of his permit in such a way was just for show and for the soldier's amusement, the Israeli army ensured Hamouda was blacklisted and taken off the sophisticated computer system that handles all Palestinian permits for the checkpoints.

Hamouda, still grieving only days after his brother's death, says all he wants to do is live a quiet life and help his parents with the family income – with his brother gone, it's needed more than ever. With one income lost, and Hamouda's income stream taken away with the destruction and termination of his permit, life has never seemed so upsetting and tough. He's been robbed of his brother, livelihood, and any future he had, he says.

"We are disposable to Israel, to their companies. So many people need jobs," he says. "I didn't want to work in the settlements, especially doing this type of job [construction], but there is no work, I didn't feel I had a choice. I have a family. We have to work, there is no work here. You know some Palestinians have built prisons for Israel, the very same prisons they were then imprisoned in when the army came and took them from their homes in the night. This is what our situation has become. It is part of the occupation, they use us, in every way."

Job security, or the lack of it, is a recurring theme for Palestinian settlement workers who can be fired by their employers at a whim, or even, such as in Hamouda's case, have their permits terminated by the government through no fault of their own. Employers, middlemen, and the Israeli government, all know individual workers are disposable – it's not hard to find a replacement, they are literally queuing up outside the settlements at dawn.

With an unemployment rate that floats around 15–20 percent and a youth unemployment rate much nearer to 30 percent, a job and a wage has become something of a luxury, especially for a group where two thirds of its population is under 30 (ILO, 2015). You'd be hard pressed to find any Palestinian worker who enjoys or wants to work in the settlements. "It's not a choice," or "I'm forced to work there," are words echoed up and down the West Bank by settlement workers who overwhelmingly say that if they could find any form of employment in Palestinian Authority areas they would put down their work boots and leave the settlements in an instant (Sbeih, 2011).

Settlement employers are all too aware of the employment and economic problems faced by the occupied Palestinian population, which allows them to exploit workers so easily, and yet still, have an unemployed reservoir of workers waiting in the wings for employment despite this. A reality is created, therefore, where workers can be fired without employers worrying about the effects on production because a new worker can be employed quickly and easily. Consequently, due to the ease in which this can be done, and the significant number of workers available, both skilled and unskilled, employers can, and do, fire workers for miniscule misdemeanors. Being late once, even if through no fault of the worker (for example by being held up at a checkpoint), asking for a raise, speaking out against the employer, having a family member killed by Israeli soldiers or trying to organise colleagues and form a trade union, can all result in dismissal. Or, it can be done simply on supply and demand, hiring and firing depending on production needs, and all without the worry of severance pay as the Israeli government continues to look the other way and actively avoid enforcing the law, something the State Comptroller has reported on numerous occasions (see for example: State Comptroller, 2011; 2013). As one construction worker[3] remarked, "If they just decided they don't like you, they don't like your face, they can fire you."

A cheap workforce and a government subsidy

Palestinian workers in the settlements, as non-citizens of the Israeli state and occupied individuals in the West Bank, are, it seems in the eyes of employers and the State of Israel, exceptions to the very labour laws that are there to protect them. This is through no fault of their own but rather through the purposeful lack of enforcement and negligence of government, and the blatant profiteering of settlement employers. That is to say, employers neglect their duty to Palestinian workers and refuse to honour their rights, as the rule rather than the exception.[4] The state not only looks the other way, and by doing so encourages the behavior, but has also been largely absent in regards to inspections and enforcement of the law when it comes to protecting Palestinian workers in comparison to their Israeli counterparts, and has never had any desire to. In the very few cases that inspectors actually respond to complaints of exploitation and rights abuses, there has been "no action taken against the companies" (Kav LaOved, 2013). Palestinian workers are left exploited, while the state although aware of it, continues to allow it, in effect giving companies and private individuals a subsidy of sorts for doing business in the settlements. That subsidy is cheap labour.

With no enforcement of the law, the vast majority of Palestinians working in the settlements leave at the end of the day with nowhere near the equivalent of the minimum wage for a day's work, with the notable exception of middlemen, who take home larger wages than the workers they employ, often skimming workers' wages to supplement or create their own depending on the agreement made between them and the employer. For workers, wages can be as little as 60 NIS for a long day's shift in the agriculture settlements, while 150 NIS is in general one of the highest wages available – still 65 NIS lower than the minimum required legally for a day's work for a full time worker. Most workers' wages appear to lie between both, however wages as low as five NIS an hour have been recorded.[5] The practice of paying less than the legal minimum wage to Palestinian workers is epidemic in the settlements. A 1970 government resolution makes clear that Palestinian workers employed in Israel must be paid and are entitled to be paid, "gross and net wages equal to the wages of any other worker in Israel with the same professional and personal particulars."[6] By 1982, this resolution was to be applied in the settlements through a military order issued stating that settlement employers were obligated to pay the workers they employed – including West Bank Palestinians as noncitizens of Israel – the Israeli minimum wage.[7] More recently, in 2007, the Israeli High Court of Justice (HCJ) ruled in a unani-

mous decision that all Israeli employers operating in the settlements in the West Bank must comply with Israeli law regarding
their employees. The ruling sought to remove any doubt that
the settlements were in any way exempted from the labour laws
that already existed to protect workers in Israel – such as entitle-
ment to minimum wage, severance pay, holiday pay, compensation for work accidents and subsequent treatment. In a display
of startling arrogance in the wake of the 2007 HCJ ruling, and
worried that workers could take them to court over the unlawful
wages they were being paid, most employers who were providing pay slips to workers in the first place just ceased the practice
(Kav LaOved, 2012: 40). Now for the Jordan Valley settlements,
more than 90 percent of employers don't provide pay slips or
any documents proving work in the settlements.[8] Some employers will employ a worker but not even apply for the relevant
permits so that worker has to enter the settlement illegally – the
worker therefore has no permit to prove they were even working,
which ends any chance of them being able to take their employer
to court over any potential labour dispute in the future. As one
lawyer[9] remarked, "It allows the employer to say, 'I don't know
this person, who is this? I've never seen them before.'" The
employer is protected. Rather than abide by the law, employers
have instead just adapted to it by concealing or stopping the production of any evidence showing unlawful practice. One Israeli
lawyer who represents Palestinian workers at the HCJ described
the whole situation of employers attempting to avoid evidence
of wrongdoing, as a "circus," where employers do all they can
to stop any future legal battle by paying workers in cash to avoid
documentation, or refusing to have any documents in Hebrew
translated into Arabic so workers cannot read the terms of

contract, don't know what they are signing, or what their rights are.[10] Employers may even get workers to sign contracts saying they will not seek compensation for injuries obtained while working or if they are dismissed from their job.[11] A solid legal basis exists to protect all workers who are employed in the settlements, regardless of whether they are Israeli, West Bank Palestinian, or a foreign citizen, yet despite this, and the state being well-aware and informed of the exploitation of Palestinian settlement workers though numerous NGO reports, court cases, and State Comptroller annual reports, little to no effective enforcement of the law exists. This allows employers to willingly get away with the economic exploitation of their workforce through, for example, not providing pay slips, written contracts,[12] or through putting false reports of hours and days worked on these documents, using the permit regime as a bargaining chip to continue exploitation, and using Palestinian middlemen to enforce and execute illegal practices.

Workers without an Israeli father or a Palestinian mother

Palestinian settlement workers feel abandoned. By their employers, by government, and by the law. A few years ago a Palestinian fieldworker who had, in her time working for Israeli workers' rights organisation Kav LaOved, carried out hundreds of interviews with Palestinian settlement workers, summed up the feeling of many of those workers succinctly. Because Israel failed to fulfill its role under the law by not monitoring safety conditions, wages and labour accidents, settlement workers, she said, had no "Israeli father." And with the Palestinian Authority's boycott of the settlements and settlement work, and unwillingness to provide settlement workers with services other Palestinian workers have, neither did they have a "Palestinian mother." Settlement workers are, it seems, the abandoned and abused kid stuck in the middle.

The Israeli father

The Israeli state has never made a conscious or concerted effort to clamp down on the exploitation of Palestinian workers in the settlements. Even the High Court of Justice ruling in 2007 that stipulated that Israeli employers in the settlements must comply with Israeli labour law, had in fact been vehemently argued *against* by the state for the 12-year-long duration of the case.[13] The state, instead, argued that Israeli labour law should not apply in the settlements for Palestinian workers, but rather that Jordanian labour law should and does due to Jordan's previous control of the West Bank prior to the 1967 occupation – a legal framework that would not protect even basic workers' rights such as minimum wage and severance pay. The attempts by the state to create a legal ambiguity over what rights Palestinian settlement workers have, has allowed settlement employers to exploit the "ambiguity of settlements under Israeli law to employ Palestinian workers under worse conditions than they would be able to employ Israelis" (Human Rights Watch, 2016: 87). The state doesn't just ignore the exploitation of settlement workers, but it has in the past, and continues to do so through an absence of enforcement, fiercely fought against the whole concept of those workers having the same basic rights and protections as Israeli workers in the first place. It comes as no surprise then that the government organs charged with enforcing the law and legal rights of Palestinian workers, the Ministry of Industry, Trade and Labor, and the Employment Staff Officer in the Civil Administration, "almost never deal with complaints submitted to them about violations against workers and do not conduct procedures of routine monitoring and supervision of employers in the West Bank to make sure they uphold workers' rights and deter violations" (Kav LaOved, 2012: 38). The Civil Administration, which is responsible for granting permits to employers for their Palestinian workers, has even been reported as having stopped the issue of paper copies of permits to workers in some settlements effectively denying those workers from one of the very few pieces of evidence they could bring to any labour dispute in court.[14] Furthermore, despite all checkpoints having a sophisticated computer system that shows when every permit-holder enters and leaves a settlement checkpoint, the Ministry of Defense has refused to provide that information during legal challenges despite numerous requests (Ibid: 33). Such information could prove beyond doubt the exact number of days and hours an employee was working, invaluable in any court case, for example to reclaim money owed due to an employer paying less than minimum wage and covering this up through producing false reports on the pay slips they submit to the Payment Division. Israel's Payment Division itself has even been scolded by the State Comptroller for accepting declarations by employers that are clearly tampered with (State Comptroller, 2014). The state has even found a way to protect companies from any lawsuits they do lose by ensuring any court rulings have "no effect" on a company's business ratings, and "that the multitude of lawsuits is referred to as 'warning information' only" (Kav LaOved, 2013: 3). A company's customers, investors, and suppliers are none the wiser that the company they deal with has been violating labour law.

It isn't an anomaly of one department letting down Palestinian settlement workers; it is a systematic and intentional action across all state departments that deal with settlement workers in one form or another. As a result of this, employers have been able to create and sustain work environments in the settlements where Palestinian workers are exploited, abused, and where there exists risks posed to their health and safety. A third of Palestinian settlement workers have also reported psychological violence, over a quarter racist or religious abuse against them, and 7 percent say they have been exposed to physical violence from their employer (Sbeih, 2011).

While laws do exist, they really only do so on paper. There is little to no effort by the state to improve working conditions in settlements for Palestinian workers, deter violations, uphold workers' rights, and in anyway stop the extreme and very obvious exploitation of the Palestinian workforce. Enforcement of the law is 'largely absent' (ILO, 2015: 26). Palestinian workers don't believe this situation will change any time soon, with one worker remarking that he couldn't see why the Israeli government would enforce the law or care about Palestinian workers' rights when the government is happy to continue a crippling occupation where Palestinians are killed regularly in the West Bank.[15] Incredibly, the Ministry of the Economy in 2013 even told a Knesset committee[16] that when it comes to workplace health and safety oversight "it carries out no activities in settlements because it does not know which law to apply" (Human Rights Watch, 2016: 93). Settlement employers therefore have nothing to deter them from continuing harsh exploitation, and using Palestinians as a cheap workforce to make as much profit as possible. Cutting corners to save money, such as not providing safety equipment or training in hazardous environments, comes at the expense of workers' health, bodies, and sometimes lives. Yet ultimately, the costs saved from rejecting the health and safety of Palestinian workers, is greater than the costs paid for those workers being injured. Injuries may be common, but getting compensation for them is difficult, lengthy, requires a costly lawyer, and is heavily skewed in the favour of the employer. Even if a worker was working legally in the settlement, had a permit, has witnesses to testify on their behalf (particularly hard as other workers fear losing their jobs and being blacklisted if they testify in court) and can prove they were working on the day of the accident, a verdict can take as many as six to ten years to be settled. A typical Palestinian settlement worker, whether injured and out of work or not, who has a family to feed, and who very likely will have been blacklisted and unable to get settlement work again because they have taken a case to court, does not have six years to wait for a verdict. Because of this, almost all cases end in a compromise where the money granted to the worker as compensation is far lower than what they would get if they continued proceedings until the end of the judicial process.[17] Employers in the end, who only pay out small sums, have little to deter them from stopping further accidents and continue as they were, as though the case, and accident, never happened.

If it's true that a society can be judged on how it treats its vulnerable and weak, the way an employer treats their injured workers can be just as telling. Setting the difficulties of financial compensation for injury aside in the aftermath of a work accident, the very treatment of workers by some employers when injury occurs is appalling. Any Palestinian settlement worker injured on the job is entitled by law to medical care in an Israeli hospital. This is especially important to consider as there exists a severe lack of funding, specialists and resources, in Palestinian Authority hospitals, where medical staff often do not have the equipment or ability to carry out the treatment needed for serious injuries.[18] Despite this, employers have refused to call ambulances for injured workers, told workers with serious injuries to "just go home," and it is not uncommon for employers to simply dump workers at the entrance to the settlements where they work and tell them to sort themselves out.[19] In the case of one worker[20] who was employed in a factory making sweets in Mishor Adumim, negligence on behalf of the employer and then the Israeli ambulance service resulted in it taking over seven hours for him to get the treatment he needed, which resulted in the permanent disability of his hand. After having his arm sucked into one of the machines at the factory and mangled, the worker had his limb inside the machine for half an hour before the employer – who refused to call an ambulance, most likely hoping to avoid any record of the work accident – got the worker out of the machine and then drove him to a PA clinic in Izariya, a town in joint Israeli-Palestinian controlled Area B. It was only after Palestinian medical staff at the PA clinic said they could not help the injured worker, that the employer eventually phoned the Israeli Magen David Adom (Israel's national ambulance service) which in a stunning failure of duty of care, then took the worker to the ill-equipped Palestinian al-Maqassid hospital. With no one at the hospital able to perform the surgery to reform his arm and hand, the worker was finally sent to the well-funded and well-equipped Hadassah hospital in West Jerusalem, just 18 miles from Mishor Adumim, the site of the work accident. Seven hours after the injury, and the worker had finally arrived in the hospital that he should have been taken to in the first place. By this time however, it was too late to bring much function back into his hand. The worker has been unable to find employment in the months following the accident.

Israeli workers' rights NGO Kav LaOved claims that "the intentional discrimination against Palestinian workers in the settlements goes on to the point of suspected contempt of court" (Kav LaOved, 2013: 2). That contempt of court vis-à-vis the labour rights of Palestinians should not just be limited to settler employers, but the state itself, which appears to see the exploitation of Palestinian settlement workers as outside the law, and which refuses to apply HCJ rulings.

Unionisation

Palestinian settlement workers may, on paper at least if not in reality, come under the remit of Israeli labour laws. They are not, however, represented by the *Histadrut*, Israel's trade union federation. While Palestinian trade unions such as the Palestinian General Federation for Trade Unions (PGFTU) lie outside of any Palestinian Authority control, they have no authority or leverage in the settlements. Attempts have been made by both workers independently and non-government-affiliated workers' rights organisations to empower Palestinian workers in the settlements, educate them on their rights, and seek to organise them into units that can then wield bargaining power over their employers.[21] However, as the settlements sit in a space where labour law is not enforced properly, or at all in most cases, employers have responded to attempts at unionisation with the dismissal of workers attempting it. This has been so successful that one of the largest surveys carried out with Palestinian settlement workers found that 93 percent had absolutely no organisation representing them (Sbeih, 2011). With the occupied Palestinian territories having

such a high unemployment rate, and with thousands of workers needing jobs, and little to no implementation of labour law
to protect workers from unfair dismissal, the bargaining power
of strike action for workers is lost – employers can simply get rid
of dissenters without much worry for legal action and severance
pay, and without much impact on production as new workers
can be picked up easily. Mass dismissal like this happens. Workers in Barkan industrial zone, who were paid 12 NIS an hour and
often worked 13 hour days, refused to sign a document from their
employer that falsely stated they were being paid minimum wage.
All who refused were fired on the spot (Kav LaOved, 2012: 42).
The permit regime need not even cause much hassle in slowing
down the employment process – middlemen can pick up workers from labour markets who may already have permits, while
thousands of workers already travel illegally and without Israeli
permits and permission for work anyway.

The Palestinian mother

The settlements, built on annexed Palestinian land, deemed illegal under international law, and an important part of Israel's control structure of the occupied West Bank, are, unsurprisingly, not
seen as legitimate by Palestinians, Palestinian led-organisations
and movements, or the Palestinian Authority. A boycott of them,
as part of the wider Boycott, Divestment, and Sanctions movement (BDS) is the general policy of the PA, including a PA ban
of working in the settlements that has been in place since 2010.
This ban stipulates that Palestinians found to be working in
the settlements could face up to five years' imprisonment if
they continued to work there. The PA has never managed to
implement this ban in any form as they are unable to provide

alternative employment to the tens of thousands of permanent and temporary Palestinians workers who rely on settlement work to survive[22] – the vast majority of whom would
leave their employment if there was an alternative waiting for
them in PA areas. The director of the PGFTU remarked that
even if the PA banned all Palestinian workers from the settlements, there would be 100,000 ready to take their place the next
day.[23] As long as occupation continues and control over trade,
Palestinian land, water, infrastructure, and the Palestinian economy, lies with Israel, the PA cannot possibly create enough alternative work. A boycott of settlement work (not to be confused
with a boycott of settlement products) is, and can only be, until
alternatives exist, just rhetorical. It serves no use to workers who
are already exploited as a cheap labour force, routinely denied
their rights enshrined in Israeli law leaving them vulnerable to
employer abuse and who do not have access to services Palestinian workers in PA controlled areas have, such as medical
insurance.[24] If anything, the boycott of settlement work alien-
ates settlement workers further from wider Palestinian society by positioning them as part of the problem rather than as
victims of occupation.

PART II

Exploiting the 'Enemy'

SIX | Segregating the labour market, stifling the economy

The segregated labour market: Palestinians as second-class workers

West Bank Palestinians working in the settlements are used as a cheap and easily exploitable blue-collar workforce, but the use of Palestinian workers in such a way is not new. Historically, these workers, both Israeli-Palestinian citizens, as well as non-citizen Palestinian workers from Gaza and the West Bank, have been funneled into specific job sectors in the Israeli labour market so they can be employed in intensive manual work such as construction and agriculture in the secondary (read: blue-collar) labour market. Job sectors that employers find difficulty employing Israeli citizens in because they are sectors that are seen as providing undesirable forms of work. The permit regime for West Bank workers to be legally employed within the Israeli labour market (Israel and the settlements) is geared specifically towards continuing this segregation between Israelis and Palestinians, where West Bank Palestinian employment is only allowed in Israel and the settlements when it is restricted to the agriculture, construction, and service sectors. Workers can therefore only get permits, and employers can only apply for those permits if the work is in the secondary labour market (Kav LaOved, 2012; ILO, 2015).

The segregation of the labour market existed long before the Oslo Accords as well as before the 1967 occupation of the Palestinian territories (Lustick, 1980; Shafir, 1989). Albeit before occupation it was Palestinian citizens of Israel that were mainly used by employers to undertake blue-collar work, these citizens being systematically cut off from other professions through the stipulation that previous army service (Palestinian citizens of Israel are not part of the country's compulsory conscription policy)[1] was a condition for employment in many white-collar, better-paid, professions; something that continues to be the case in the present day. It's why a very small number of Israeli-Palestinian citizens, around 3,000, have even volunteered for service in the IDF – in direct opposition to their Palestinian community – in an attempt to better set themselves up for future employment (Kanaaneh, 2008). Palestinians in Israel have always had a very low social, political, and economic status (Pappe, 2011). Discrimination against them is rife, indeed the very discriminatory nature of the Israeli state (politically and socially) which places Jewish citizens above Palestinian-citizens as a core part of Zionist ideology, has had the knock-on impact on who Israeli employers wish to choose for employment opportunities (Miaari, Zussman and Zussman, 2010). Furthermore, Israeli government funds are disproportionately allocated to Israeli-Jewish communities in the country, leaving their Israeli-Palestinian counterparts underfunded and underdeveloped. The effects of this has resulted in Israeli-Jewish communities and its residents having better educational opportunities, services, and consequently job opportunities, primarily gaining employment in the primary labour market, unlike Israeli-Palestinian citizens who have found themselves positioned in the secondary labour market.[2]

The occupation of the Palestinian territories in 1967 did how-ever bring about a change in regards to which group the state and Israeli employers would primarily funnel into the secondary labour market. Israeli military orders drawn up in the immedi-ate aftermath of the occupation looked to subsume and control the Palestinian economy and workforce into the Israeli economy, and create an easily accessible and cheap workforce that could be utilised in regards to Israeli production needs (Samara, 1988). It was an intentional, policy-directed move. With this sudden avail-ability to Israeli employers of an occupied, suppressed, and low-income population, non-citizen West Bank Palestinians began to replace citizen Israeli-Palestinians in the lowest status and worst paid jobs. These workers' non-citizen status was sought-after in particular due to their lack of political rights, and thus potential for cheaper employment and greater exploitation compared to state citizens who had more protection and less ambiguity under the law. The working class, the West Bank *proletariat* that made a living from the land, suffered the most from the occupation as their workspace and land was annexed and their livelihoods stripped and taken from them as Israeli occupation bedded in. The result was that many in these rural communities became dependent on work in the Israeli labour market.

With the work permit regime implemented during the early 1990s, which stipulated that all West Bank Palestinians working in Israel must be granted a permit to do so,[3] the segregation of the Israeli labour market with West Bank Palestinians in blue-collar work became cemented through actual policy. Now, the funneling of these workers into employment sectors such as agri-cultural and construction came directly from the top. These were jobs that West Bank Palestinians were previously employed in,

however the onset of the work permit regime put this segregation into law. There are no exceptions to the designated sectors
West Bank Palestinians are and are not allowed to work in. In one
case, an Israeli employer who had been searching for two years
for a skilled carpenter – and who was unable to find a suitable
Israeli citizen as a candidate in that time – discovered a talented
West Bank Palestinian carpenter who fit the bill. An application
for a permit was rejected numerous times, however, because car-
pentry wasn't included in the list of jobs permitted for Palestinian labourers to gain a work permit. The case, which garnered
government attention, was eventually shut down by the Ministry
of Industry, Trade, and Labor, who asserted that the employer
should get the skilled labourer they required from Romania not
the West Bank, despite the obvious illogical geographical, and
costly, problems associated with this (Kav LaOved, 2012: 8).
The permit regime not only put into law this segregation but also
effectively ended the flow of labour as functioning completely
as supply- and demand-based, instead creating a system where
its control also depended on the military and its considerations
(Farsakh, 2002: 16) and therefore where Palestinian labour flow
could be restricted to certain geographical areas or stopped
completely through implementing closure policies on the West
Bank.[4]

A state policy created segregated labour market
Studies on labour market segregation tend to solely attribute segregation to the economic interests of capitalists (Bonacich, 1972;
Peck, 1989). Reich, Gordon, and Edwards (1973), for example,
see it as a tactic of 'divide and rule' in order to ensure continued
hegemony of the economic system. However these studies fail to

consider the full possibilities within an occupying state and the territories it is occupying, and the consequent complex political environment that is a result, never mind the potential ideological reasons that may fuel such an occupation – in this case, Zionism. When analysing the context of the two segregated labour markets (primary and secondary) within the Israeli economy, however, it is possible to see that they have been formulated through a series of stages manifesting partially from the political statuses of the constituent populations *as well as* state mechanisms of economic incorporation since the formation of the state, rather than primarily through market forces (Rosenhek, 2003). Couple this with the known and widespread discrimination of Palestinians by Israeli employers, due primarily to the influence of Zionist ideology, and a path is illustrated showing the importance of the state and state rhetoric in formulating and advancing this market segregation. That is, discrimination against Palestinians in Israeli society as a whole for their being Palestinian cemented and encouraged the separation of Palestinians (citizen and non-citizen) from Israeli-Jewish citizens in the labour market, which has been strengthened further by state policies, particularly with the advent of the work permit regime. Israeli government policies have, along with discrimination, played a significant part in anchoring the Palestinian economy within the Israeli economy, taking advantage of the occupied Palestinian population as well as making a concerted effort to immerse the West Bank Palestinian workforce into low-status employment (Farsakh, 2002). This can be seen most clearly with the way that the Israeli government dealt with the Gaza Strip in comparison to the West Bank during the Oslo Accords peace process, where there was a clear effort to hold onto more control around labour flow, economy, and trade in the

West Bank, than there was with Gaza.[5] Economic policy was, in fact, to effectively sever ties with Gaza, while on the other hand, incorporate the West Bank economy further and strengthen easy access to the cheap Palestinian workforce there.

While Israel's primary reason for holding on to the West Bank may be territorial, the dealings with the native Palestinian population as part of the occupation has looked to create and utilise that easily exploitable cheap blue-collar workforce as a benefit of Israeli occupation. The subsequent expansion of Israeli settlements in regards to that territorial aim, has, in turn, been bolstered physically and economically by the presence of this low-status, exploitable workforce, that is only allowed to work in employment sectors that settlement businesses would struggle to get Israeli citizens to work in anyway. Even with the advent of foreign migrant workers in Israel during the 1990s, and therefore the introduction of another cheap and potentially exploitable workforce, settlement worker numbers remained relatively stable,[6] as settlement companies took advantage of West Bank Palestinian workers' close proximity to their worksites, but also crucially to the ambiguity – encouraged and fostered by the Israeli government – around West Bank Palestinian workers' legal status and rights that had become a central tenet of employing Palestinian workers in the settlements (see Chapter 5). Such ambiguity did not exist to the same extent with foreign migrant workers.

The result of all of this has been the creation of an overlap between class (low) and ethnicity (Palestinian) in the labour market that has continued to be reinforced and built on through state policies and society-wide discrimination. Israeli-Palestinian citizens are limited because of discrimination due to their ethnicity and non-participation in the military; but crucially they are not, at least by law anyway, restricted to certain employment sectors. West Bank Palestinians, as a state-suppressed and occupied population, have, however, been used specifically to fill employment gaps in sectors that the vast majority of Israelis (specifically Israeli-Jewish citizens who occupy a higher social status in society than Israeli-Palestinians[7]) do not apply for or want to apply for. The settlements show this funneling of Palestinian West Bank workers into blue-collar work most clearly. Factories with their labour intensive, low-waged jobs move specifically to the settlements in order to capitalise on the proximity of not just a cheap and easily exploitable workforce but also a large workforce that is willing to work in these undesirable jobs (Human Rights Watch, 2016). It's why settlement farms are able to cultivate over 9,000 hectares of land, and there are 20 industrial settlement zones and over 1,000 Israeli factories situated in the settlements rather than elsewhere. Settlers, who make up around half of all workers employed in the settlements and who cannot be so easily exploited, are overwhelmingly employed out with farms and factories, with less than 7.5 percent of settlers working in traditional blue-collar employment such as farming, quarrying, mining, and similar (Ibid: 106). While the settlers that are working in such employment almost always work in bureaucratic and management positions within those sectors and not the manual labour aspects.

Stifling the Palestinian economy and controlling Area C

Segmenting the labour force and positioning non-citizen Palestinian labourers as a cheap and exploitable workforce for Israeli producers and businesses can only work, however, if opportunities for Palestinian development are stifled to the extent that job creation within the Palestinian Authority areas can never meet the demand of Palestinians, nor dig into the unemployed pool of labourers sufficiently enough to affect the ever-fluctuating supply and demand needs of Israeli employers.[8] Although Israel's primary reason for the occupation of the West Bank is due to its territorial ambitions for a greater *Eretz Israel*,[9] controlling the West Bank economy and creating a dependence on the Israeli economy has been a significant factor in consolidating further control out with the more tangible military aspects of occupation. Stifling the development of Palestinian urban centers, and creating a dependent market on Israeli products also brings a beneficial economic dimension to what is, in reality, a costly military and state endeavour.

While effort had been made in the years following occupation to subsume the Palestinian economy, market, and labour force into the Israeli economy, it was with the Paris Protocol, signed in April 1994[10] – an economic framework that came in the aftermath, and was a result of, the Oslo Accords – that cemented this dependence. The Protocol determined the New Israeli Shekel (NIS) as the main legal tender in the West Bank,[11] imposed draconian restrictions on the movement of goods in and out of the Palestinian territories, and gave Israel de facto control of those movements and what products were allowed or not allowed and to what numbers, as well as creating a joint economic committee that gave, in reality, Israel the power to veto any Palestinian Authority requests they deemed as not in their economic benefit. Israel frequently uses everything in its economic arsenal to thwart any Palestinian attempts to either improve the Palestinian economy or improve the status of the Palestinian population as a whole. As an example, when the Palestinian Authority first began steps to join the International Criminal Court at the beginning of 2015 – a move which could pave the way to prosecute Israelis for war crimes – Israel begun to withhold clearance revenues from the Palestinian Authority.[12] Under the Paris Protocol, Israel was charged with collecting taxes[13] (termed 'clearance revenues') on behalf of the Palestinian Authority. Those revenues, crucial for the payment of wages to tens of thousands of Palestinian civil servants, were to be turned over to the Palestinian Authority every year. Such as in this case, the Israeli government frequently delays, or withholds these payments in an attempt to gain leverage. The Paris Protocol, an interim economic framework that was intended to last just five years, continues to dictate the economic relationship between Israel and the Palestinian Authority, to the latter's detriment, more than two decades later.

For any form of sustainable economic development, the West Bank and its producers need access to markets. Israel controls all borders surrounding the West Bank, including the border between the West Bank and Jordan. It also controls all trade going in and out,[14] which has led to two thirds of the occupied Palestinian territories' imports coming from Israeli producers, as well as 87 percent of its exports going to the Israeli market (ILO, 2015: 16). With the Paris Protocol, Israel continues to control what markets are open to Palestinian producers, and what products are allowed.[15] With Israeli occupation controlling business, trade, and land, West Bank Palestinian capitalists have only one real route for money-making – to work with the Israeli business class in the marketing of Israeli products in the occupied and Israeli-controlled West Bank market (Samara, 2000: 118–9). The initial months and years of the occupation didn't just create a dependence from the rural West Bank Palestinian working class on the

Israeli labour market, but also a dependence from the West Bank business class on the Israeli economy, who could only trade with, and often only market, Israeli products. Arab nations that had previously had an export/import role before occupation became completely cut off by Israeli-implemented economic policies that shut the door on Palestinian trade to them. The land wasn't just occupied; the Palestinian economy was too.

The impact that Israeli policies and occupation has had on Area C – an area that should be the economic powerhouse of any Palestinian state – has been the biggest obstacle to forging a sustainable Palestinian economy and encouraging development. The direct negative economic impact of Israel's severe restrictions on Palestinian freedom of movement, farming, and development in Area C not only affects production and employment opportunities, but as a result loses the Palestinian economy an estimated $3.4 billion a year.[16] Furthermore, Israel, in almost all cases, refuses to allow Palestinians to mine the raw materials that can be found in Area C, and the World Bank has estimated that at least $1 billion is lost every year due to this refusal (World Bank, 2013: 13). Human Rights Watch, when researching quarrying in the West Bank, found that Israel was issuing permits to Israeli and even European companies to quarry the occupied Palestinian territory, yet it had rejected every application from Palestinian companies to quarry the land in Area C since 1994, resulting in an estimated quarter of a billion USD loss for the Palestinian economy annually (Human Rights Watch, 2016).[17] Allowing the land to be developed to its full potential, however, could result in the creation of 150,000–200,000 direct and indirect jobs per 100,000 dunums (10,000 hectares), a development that would completely rejuvenate the impoverished Palestinian communities of the valley, dramatically reduce unemployment, increase spending, and give Palestinian agricultural workers the opportunity to leave the low-waged, exploitative, (perceived) shameful, and highly damaging (for themselves personally and politically) settlement farm work.

This severe inability to develop or even cultivate land has left many of the Area C Palestinian towns and villages reliant on international donors to provide basic services and infrastructure like water, schools, and even tented accommodation for families to live in (OCHA, 2014a) – accommodation that, despite coming from organisations such as the European Union, is frequently bulldozed down by the IDF (Hass, 2016). In the start of 2016 just 1.5 percent of Palestinian applications for development in Area C were approved (OCHA, 2016), and in between 2000 and 2012, of the 3565 applications submitted, only 210 got the go-ahead (Human Rights Watch, 2016: 37). On the other hand Israeli settlers in the valley build frequently and without the relevant permissions, being granted that permission retroactively (Halper and Schaeffer, 2012). The discrimination is as startling and obvious as the negative consequences are for Palestinian development and growth in Area C.

Although Area C is the area most deeply affected by the inability to develop and build infrastructure, there are knock-on effects to Palestinian communities in both Area A and B. The way the West Bank has been split up as a result of the Oslo Accords has resulted in small islands of Palestinian (PA) controlled areas, surrounded by oceans of Israeli controlled areas. Palestinian urban centers have been effectively cut off from each other by Area C land that encircles and bantustanises the West Bank. Palestinian towns and cities cannot, therefore, effectively connect major infrastructure projects to each other because the Israeli military controls the land in between and refuses, in almost all cases, to allow Palestinian building work – for example new roads or water networks – on it.

Strengthening the occupation, benefitting the settlements

Israeli policy, by subsuming the Palestinian economy, controlling trade, and exploiting the resources of the occupied territory for its own population and against international law,[18] has not just tied the Palestinian economy to Israel's, but made it dependent on it, stifling any potential for Palestinian development. Neither the Palestinian Authority, nor private individuals and investors can substantially develop the West Bank or use its natural resources while under such conditions, and therefore there are very few opportunities to create jobs for a population group that continues, and has done for years, suffered from high poverty and unemployment rates. The World Bank, unsurprisingly, has described the West Bank economy as unsustainable, stating that the crippling Israeli restrictions on development are the primary obstruction to investing in Palestine (World Bank, 2012: 4). With Palestinian rural areas being affected most greatly by Israel's control of the land, Area C residents have particularly suffered, many losing their traditional farming and herding livelihood. Without development opportunities, or being able to use the land to build or farm on, the only choice for tens of thousands of workers has been to find work in blue-collar jobs in the Israeli labour market. On the other hand, settlers and Israeli settlement businesses have benefitted from the Palestinians' loss, and have been actively encouraged by the Israeli government to move to the settlements through generous financial benefits and tax breaks.

This has included the state designating 90 settlements and virtually all of the settlement industrial zones as *National Priority Areas,* entitling the businesses and civilians who live there a series of government subsidies.[19] This is on top of the benefits of operating in a zone – the settlements – that has in effect been deemed outside of the law in regards to upholding the workers' rights of Palestinians (see Chapter 5). It's not just cheap to employ the neighbouring suppressed Palestinian workforce, there is also the direct benefit of government subsidies, as well as the indirect benefit of a lack of state enforcement of Palestinian workers' rights – which for example, allows employers to save money on safety equipment, training, and providing adequate working facilities, without much worry for having to pay compensation for injuries that occur. In total, this has led to the cost of hiring an Israeli citizen worker in the settlements to be 2,000 NIS a month *more* than hiring a non-citizen West Bank Palestinian worker (Human Rights Watch, 2016: 92) – a reality that has given settlement businesses a significant advantage over their non-settlement counterparts (State Comptroller, 2012: 1677), and gives, in effect, a further subsidy (cheap labour, often cheaper than the legal minimum wage) to businesses operating in the settlements.

While the West Bank economy has been suppressed and subsumed and its people have suffered, the settlements' economies have been boosted, their populations have benefitted, and they are given every possible opportunity to flourish by the Israeli government in an attempt to further cement and expand Israel's territorial conquest in the occupied West Bank.[20] The result of this has been the strengthening of the occupation on the ground, and of its control structure as land is annexed and infrastructure is built and improved between the settlements and Israel. Resources are continuously taken, and Palestinian development is severely limited. All of this contributes to the inability for Palestinians to develop employment opportunities, cultivate their own land and continue traditional livelihoods, and fosters a dependence – especially in rural Area C communities – on the Israeli labour market which has, for decades, through state policy and discrimination, funneled the Palestinian workforce towards undesirable low-paid blue-collar employment.

SEVEN | The creation of precincts of potential employment

As the Israeli government began to annex Palestinian land in the aftermath of the 1967 occupation of the West Bank and Gaza Strip, the economy was annexed in tandem, creating a weak Palestinian economy with complete dependence on a dominant Israeli one. As discussed in Chapter 6, Israeli policy in the West Bank has been to give the Palestinian Authority little to no opportunity to properly develop or industrialise the West Bank, use its resources, and therefore potentially provide employment opportunities to the hundreds of thousands of unemployed Palestinians and consequently improve the economic wellbeing of the population as a whole.[1] The significance of Israeli policy on the Palestinian economy is important in regards to Palestinian settlement workers as the Palestinian Authority under such constraints simply cannot provide any alternative employment to the tens of thousands of Palestinians employed in the settlements – workers who overwhelmingly say they are forced into this work in order to survive and put food on the table. Neither is there much opportunity for private investors, or indeed want from them, to invest in the West Bank and subsequently aid in job creation when the West Bank market, labour force, resources, and exports and imports are all controlled by Israel and Israeli government policies, and not for the benefit of the

Palestinians or their economy. It is a highly risky and unpredictable environment for investors.

Although the Palestinian Authority cannot create enough alternative jobs for settlement workers to be able to put down their tools and leave the illegal settlements, crucially, even if the Palestinian Authority could, or a worker themselves found employment elsewhere in the West Bank, the conditions of occupation would severely limit that worker's ability to be able to take up such employment anyway. Israel has created multiple obstacles, both physical and bureaucratic, that impede Palestinian movement internally in the West Bank. The Wall, Israeli army checkpoints (both permanent and temporary "flying" checkpoints), the permit regime, Area C firing zones, nature reserves, land under the administrative control of settlements (whether used or not), earth mounts, trenches, and roadblocks all impede Palestinian freedom of movement, and as a combined force seriously limit or even completely halt the ability to move from place to place. The occupied West Bank in reality has over 500 significant obstacles to Palestinian free movement, including 96 fixed checkpoints, of which 57 are internal,[2] many of them situated deep inside the West Bank. That is in addition to other non-physical obstacles such as the existence and concept of the Area A, B, and C system and the permit regime. Include the H2 area of Hebron, where Israeli settlements patrolled and guarded by thousands of soldiers have taken over one fifth of the city, and another further 100 obstacles, military-only zones and roads can be added to that number (OCHA, 2014b). Extreme freedom of movement restrictions are imposed on all West Bank Palestinians by the occupying army, while the creation of the settlements, settler-only roads, and the purposeful splitting up of the West Bank into three different areas of control (A, B, and C) has separated Palestinian population centers from each other, creating, in essence, a barrier to where Palestinians can even search and gain employment.

For Palestinian settlement workers, finding alternative work outside of the settlements is not just difficult due to the limited employment options, development opportunities, and huge demand for any existing jobs due to high unemployment levels, but much potential employment is out of reach completely for many because of these movement restrictions in place. Proximity to employment often becomes the prerequisite for employers rather than the employment of a person with the best ability or skillset for the job. For example, a talented carpenter in the south Hebron Hills may fit the bill for a job at a woodshop in Ramallah just 26 miles away, but with Israeli restrictions on movement, checkpoints, and road systems, the journey to get there will take several hours, will go past junctions where soldiers frequently hold up Palestinian traffic, carry out thorough and sometimes humiliating searches, and where Palestinians have been shot and killed during previous escalations in violence.[3] The roads used – and there are often only one or two roads for Palestinians leading in and out of Palestinian urban centers to ensure easy control for the IDF – can be closed by the military easily and without warning, allowing for a ramping up or down on the severity of movement restrictions.[4] It doesn't add up to an environment where a worker can guarantee getting to work every day, or get there on time, safely, or in any way affordably for low income individuals and families. In some cases, a journey of 1 kilometer has been documented as taking twenty times that distance just because of settlements, road closures and the Wall (Human Rights Watch, 2016: 58). Furthermore, over 60 kilometers of internal West Bank roads are settler-only and forbidden for Palestinians to even use. Yet on roads that Palestinians are allowed to travel on between Palestinian populated areas, the prevalence of lengthy delays, humiliating treatment, and potentially dangerous encounters, has led to Palestinian use on some main roads (which Palestinians are allowed to travel on) to be so low that the roads have become de-facto settler-only roads used only by the IDF and Israeli settlers (B'Tselem, 2015). The Wall on the other hand, described by the International Labor Organization as "the single largest obstacle to movement" for Palestinians (2015: 15) and which continues to be built over a decade after the International Court of Justice ruled that it was illegal in 2004,[5] is one of the prime examples of Israel's mechanisms of impeding Palestinian freedom of movement. The Wall,[6] which when finally complete will be 707 kilometers in length – over twice the length of the Green Line (1949 Armistice Line) – and 85 percent of which will run through the West Bank itself (OCHA, 2011: 3) – was built, according to the Israeli government, with security in mind. This reasoning however has been widely debunked. The reality is that the Wall was built as a structure to consolidate further control of the West Bank and crucially annex more Palestinian land to the 'Israeli' side and secure it for the future in regards to any future negotiations between Israel and the Palestinian Authority.[7] If security was a reason for the Wall's conception and creation, it was low down on the list. Completed parts of the Wall have already divided the West Bank into three separate parts. One in the north, which is separated by the strategically built Ariel finger, where the Wall encloses the large Israeli settlement of Ariel, which stretches 20 kilometers into the West Bank and past the Green Line, built along a ridge of hills splitting the Palestinian urban centers on both sides apart. The

second in the middle between the Ariel finger and Ma'ale Adumim
Settlement Bloc, and the third, south of this Bloc. The result of
the Wall's snaking path, therefore, does not just make movement
between the West Bank and Israel difficult, but also between the
West Bank and the West Bank. Because the Wall deviates quite
substantially from the 1949 Green Line, enclaves have been created between the Green Line and the Wall. These enclaves called
the *seam zone* are classed as Area C and have often been deemed
military zones by the Israeli army. For the approximately 33,000
West Bank Palestinians residing here (not including East Jerusalem and its residents), many from poor rural communities such
as the seam zone community of Al-Walaja, life is particularly difficult and freedom of movement severely restricted. It's not just
a case of being inconvenienced; these obstacles to movement are
severe. In some of the more isolated seam zone villages, doctors
and healthcare professionals have been prevented from accessing
the villages as they require 'visitor permits' issued by the army,
permits that are rejected frequently, and in the case of emergen-
cies often not issued fast enough. Due to such circumstances
some pregnant women living in the seam zone have been known
to leave their home weeks before their due date in order to guarantee access to a hospital, while there have even been cases of
births taking place at checkpoints (OCHA, 2011: 18).

This bantustanisation of the West Bank by Israel with Palestinian population groups split up due to the Oslo Accords Area
A, B, C system, 135 official Israeli settlements (as of 2016) and
another 100 outposts,[8] along with over 500 physical obstacles
such as Israeli army checkpoints and the devastating and snaking path of the Wall, has created a highly destructive multi-
layered control system to Palestinian freedom of movement

where the severity can be increased or decreased depending on
the whim of the Israeli military. It is a system that continues to be
consolidated and strengthened, and is designed, fundamentally,
to stop the free movement of goods and people, control Palestinian lives as much as possible, and split the West Bank up into
easily controllable pieces and thus easily controllable population
groups (Weizmann, 2007). It splits families in two, cuts Palestinian villages and towns off from basic services and infrastructure,
and rips into every facet of Palestinian life. Whereas in a West
Bank free of occupation, a civilian would hypothetically be able to
move easily from city to city, north to south, east to west, because
of Israeli occupation this is not just difficult, it is sometimes completely impossible. Israeli occupation has not just stifled movement, development, and job creation, it has also created *precincts
of potential employment* – that is, areas where Palestinians can
look for work based on their ability to travel there and potential to be able to do so regularly in the future and therefore hold
onto that employment. That ability varies from place to place,
but across the West Bank it is impossible to move freely without
Israeli government and military interference. This fragmentation
of the West Bank into hundreds of small separate Palestinian
areas is becoming more permanent as further obstacles are added
and the settlements continue to grow and expand. The status quo
is already becoming irreversible, especially considering that new
outposts set up by settlers, which are almost always added to the
existing settlement road, water, and electricity network,[9] are often
situated in such a way as to link other settlements together and
'fill the gaps' between them. These precincts of potential employment for Palestinian workers are only solidifying further as occupation continues unabated.

Since the beginning of the occupation, and certainly with the building of the Wall, the freedom of movement restrictions on West Bank Palestinians has been, thankfully, well-documented by numerous national and international NGOs as well as global governance organisations. Where the significance of Palestinian settlement workers comes into this, however, is much less highlighted. Settlement workers overwhelmingly tend to be from rural communities where the traditional herding and farming lifestyle was the primary way to carve out a living before the occupation of the West Bank and in the initial years following when less land had been annexed, there were fewer settlements and those settlements were much smaller in size. However, as the settlements grew over the years and land was taken for their expansion and/ or declared military zones, and so became forbidden to cultivate and farm on, livelihoods disappeared – and through absolutely no fault or wish of the Palestinian inhabitants. These rural communities lost their way of life, their economies crumbled, and families lost their income stream. Villagers not only lost land, but they also lost their freedom of movement at the same time. The curse of being situated beside a settlement didn't just stretch to having land stolen, it also meant that in almost all cases, the Palestinian village became, with the onset of the Oslo Accords in the 1990s, designated as Area C, and/or surrounded completely by Area C swathes of land – land under the administrative control of the settlements and Israeli military. The land couldn't be cultivated, and much of it became forbidden to enter or even walk on. Military firing areas, settlement 'buffer zones' and the settlements themselves as some examples. Ignore the occupying army's rules and risk being arrested or even fatally shot. Furthermore, any building or development work in these rural areas requires

Israeli permits and permission, which is almost impossible to get. Trying to manufacture goods becomes virtually impossible for budding entrepreneurs as raw materials are off-limits, meaning resources would have to be expensively shipped into the occupied West Bank from outside markets. The traditional lifestyle wasn't just stripped from the local population, opportunities for self-employment, entrepreneurship, and Palestinian-led industrialisation and development were also taken away. Looking outwards for employment to the more developed and urban Palestinian areas would be more of an option for rural Palestinians if occupation didn't exist and Palestinians could move freely from place to place. But then again, there would be less or no need to look there in the first place as the traditional livelihoods of thousands would not have been taken from them. The creation and continued expansion of the settlements and their related industrial and agricultural projects, however, has literally brought a form of employment to the doorstep of the rural impoverished Palestinian communities that have suffered the most from the settlements, and transformed these communities into pools of easily exploitable workers. Settlement work brings workers shame and humiliation, and makes them a part of their own nation's destruction, and that's on top of the fact that they are being exploited and used as a cheap and disposable workforce by their occupiers. Yet the draconian freedom of movement restrictions on Palestinians – especially those in Area C – prevent these workers from looking for, and gaining, employment elsewhere in the West Bank. Employment in the settlements becomes the only viable route to make an income for rural unemployed, including illegal workers, who take dangerous risks to their lives just to try and gain some form of work in the settlements near to where they live. It's not a job they want to do, or one they are proud of, but their economic need is so great, and employment options so few, that the risk becomes necessity.

The reality is that even if many other employment options existed for Palestinian workers in Palestinian Authority controlled areas, the journey for illegal workers from their village to the nearby Israeli settlement – a distance of often only a few kilometers – passing through unmanned gaps, or literally over the Wall under the cover of darkness, is for some more achievable for them to get to, and more within their economic means, than travelling to other areas of the West Bank for employment. The freedom of movement restrictions across the West Bank are *that* severe. It's why settlement employment in these rural Palestinians communities that are geographically close to settlements, became the main employment sector. It works the other way as well. Settlement employment percentage figures in Palestinian cities in Area A – and therefore Palestinian population areas that are in general not surrounded by, or such close neighbours with larger settlements, and where there is more potential for Palestinian employment opportunities – are significantly lower than in the villages that sit beside the settlements.[10] It's not that there is no need for employment in these built up areas compared to the rural ones. Unemployment rates in Palestinian urban centers, although often not as high as rural communities, still fluctuate around 15–20 percent while poverty rates are also high, especially in the cramped city refugee camps where incomes are desperately needed. But freedom of movement here, like in the rest of the West Bank, is highly limited due to Israeli control and restrictions. Palestinians are hemmed into their own areas, and thus are hemmed into certain types of employment and places where they can be employed

and look for employment. At least in Area A cities, there is room
for some development and job creation – albeit still stifled greatly
by Israel's control of the Palestinian economy – and therefore
different employment sectors may exist, including employment
that does not aid in the destruction of Palestinian self-determination aspirations in the way that settlement work does. In the
rural communities, separated from Palestinian urban centers, and
starved of their land, livelihood, and opportunities to develop,
dependency on the Israeli labour market grows – especially for
individuals whose family lost most, or all of their land. It's work
forced upon them, and that they must do in order to survive.

The case study of Az-Zubeidat

Looking at the village of Az-Zubeidat, a community touched on
in Chapter 3, is a good way of illustrating exactly how these precincts of potential employment work. The village is, by its very
nature, a rural farming community. The open land, the fertile soil,
the water resources, the natural vegetation of the valley plain and
the hills that mark its edge, are all perfect for grazing animals and
complemented by them. And Az-Zubeidat *was* a farming community, but now it really just functions as a labour source for the
agricultural settlements, mainly Argaman and its farms that surround it. Moving around the Jordan Valley as a Palestinian can be
dangerous, is difficult, and at times completely impossible. The
Valley is 90 percent Area C. Palestinian villages are cut off from
each other by military firing zones, settlements, and in the north,
minefields that still dot part of the valley. Residents frequently talk
about being scared of leaving their own villages for fear of walking
on land the Israeli military has deemed as forbidden for Palestinians, and being shot at by the heavily armed settlers and soldiers

that rule every aspect of valley and Area C life. Az-Zubeidat itself is split between Area B and C, albeit 'split' is a very misleading term. The actual cramped confines of the village where people live is designated as Area B – around 36 dunums in total. The rest of the village area, 4,087 dunums, which amounts to 99 percent of the total historical area of Az-Zubeidat, is Area C and under the complete control of the Israeli military. In essence, the village has a very tiny Palestinian urban center, while the village land surrounding it – that used to be cultivated by families here – has been annexed and is the property of the occupier.

Comprehensive surveys on the small rural villages in the West Bank are not so common, but one conducted on Az-Zubeidat in 2012 by the Applied Research Institute-Jerusalem (ARIJ) found that only 20 private cars existed in the village, along with two taxis (ARIJ, 2012), and one infrequent *service* or small bus that serves the population of 1,400 along with several other communities in the valley. Jericho, the largest Palestinian urban center in the Jordan Valley, and where there may be some employment opportunities available – for example in the service sector – lies 27 kilometers south of the village. To find a private car from the village going in that direction or public transport to get there is difficult, and on some days may not exist. Although the large regular green Israeli buses run by the *Egged* company that serve the settlements can be seen driving up and down the main highway are frequent and fast, they are forbidden for West Bank Palestinians to use. Walking to Jericho is possible, but the chances of running into Israeli army jeeps and soldiers, or coming across a flying checkpoint can be high and confrontations are not uncommon. And, of course, in the height of summer when temperatures regularly hit well-over 40 degrees Celsius, walking anywhere for that length of time can be dangerous and even fatal. All of this makes it difficult, if not completely impossible at times, to travel out of the village, and therefore hold down employment, or even look for employment further than a few kilometers either side of Az-Zubeidat. While a few residents are trying to hold onto some form of self-employment through farming where they can, when collated there exist far more people in the village (1,400) than the number of livestock collectively owned by the residents (850), which gives as good an indication as any as to how the farming and herding lifestyle is fast disappearing (ARIJ, 2012).[11] Occupation, land annexation, and an inability to travel freely has left the village with an unemployment rate that has hit 80 percent in the past. For those who are employed, 97 percent work in the agricultural sector, and the vast majority of those workers, bar a few residents who have managed to hold on to some animals and land, are employed in the settlement farms that sit beside the Palestinian village.

Notably Palestinian villages like Al-Walaja and Nahalin that are situated near large and seemingly ever-expanding settlement cities such as Ma'ale Adumim and Beitar Illit, have significant numbers of residents working in settlement construction. In Az-Zubeidat, the residents have been hemmed into the agricultural sector within settlement work as a whole. The precincts of potential employment, then, do not just dictate where employment can be gained, but can also at times dictate what form of employment takes place depending on what sort of settlement – industrial zone, agricultural, or settlements with on-going construction projects – are situated close by.

EIGHT | A reserve army of labour

> *Taking them as a whole, the general movements of wages are*
> *exclusively regulated by the expansion and contraction of the*
> *industrial reserve army, and these again correspond to the peri-*
> *odic changes of the industrial cycle. They are, therefore, not*
> *determined by the variations of the absolute number of the work-*
> *ing population, but by the varying proportions in which the*
> *working-class is divided into active and reserve army, by the*
> *increase or diminution in the relative amount of the surplus-*
> *population, by the extent to which it is now absorbed, now set free.*
> (Marx, 1867: 340)

The existence of a high supply of unemployed Palestinian blue-collar workers in the occupied West Bank has been of significant benefit to Israeli capitalists. The settlements and settlement businesses don't just have access to a large pool of unemployed non-citizen and easily exploitable workers, but that pool is also geographically concentrated near them and limited in employment options due to freedom of movement restrictions and the purposeful stifling of Palestinian development and economy by Israel. Concentrated in precincts of potential employment, many Palestinian workers in rural communities situated near the settlements depend solely on settlement work. If they are fired – which is easy for employers to do when little to no state enforcement of workers' rights exists in the settlements – there are very few other job options available to them. With unemployment rates in the West Bank high, especially in rural communities, there is a need for settlement jobs in these communities. Settlement employers, therefore, have a pool of unemployed workers always waiting for employment, be it temporary, permanent, part-time, or full-time. Production increasing is never a problem; workers can be picked up easily. If there is a production decrease, workers can just be laid off with no need to worry about compensation or trade union action. What has been created is a vulnerable workforce that can be paid very little, is heavily reliant on their occupier, and which is easily available and disposable to Israeli capitalists in the settlements.

Marx and the reserve army of labour

The incorporation of Palestinians within the Israeli economy and labour market, as discussed in Chapter 6, has been well-documented in regards to the use of Palestinian labourers as a means of cheap production. Naturally, therefore, it could be assumed that the Israeli economy would be exposed to much Marxist interpretation, but such analysis is rather limited in scope. Existing arguments drawing on Marxist thought include analysis that Israeli occupation and thus control of the Palestinian economy has divided the working classes of Israel and Palestine keeping them divided and distracted from their exploitation, as well as the argument that the central purpose of Israeli occupation is Palestinian resource and workforce exploitation (see, for example: Bishara, 2001; Hass, 2002; or Halper's concept of the 'matrix of control', 2000). Marxist theory, at its core, argues that repression exists to facilitate exploitation of the working class at the hands of the capitalist hegemony (Marx and Engels, 1848; Marx, 1867). It would be fundamentally wrong to argue that Israeli occupation and the settlement project, driven by Zionist ideology over the decades, exists simply to exploit Palestinian non-citizens and/or the resources of the Palestinian territories – although without doubt this has become a welcome benefit of occupation. By wielding the explanatory potential from Karl Marx's concept of a *reserve army of labour*, that is the use of an easily accessible pool of unemployed blue-collar labourers for cheap rates of production who can easily be made redundant when demand is low, and easily employed when demand is high, important insights can be provided into the relationship between Palestinian non-citizen workers and their employment in the Israeli settlements. It appears that just one study (Farjoun, 1984) touches on this Marxist concept in relation to Palestinian non-citizen labour previously, albeit within Israel rather than the settlements specifically. Although insightful in its scope, there remain flaws within Farjoun's analysis. The study argued that non-citizen Palestinians working within Israel are made redundant by Israeli companies when demand is low, thus avoiding the dismissal of any Jewish-Israeli workers; conversely when demand is high, the Palestinian workforce is employed again. The conclusion is therefore that the non-citizen labour force has "its absolute dependence on market forces" (1984, 90). However, as discussed in Chapter 6 and 7, it's possible to conclude that the workforce elasticity of Palestinian non-citizen labour can, has, and continues to be, dictated by state policy, *as well* as, market forces.

Marxists would put class above other forms of identity as the most important factor between the Israeli and Palestinian populations. Within the context of the Israel/Palestine conflict, however, and the very nature of the Israeli state as one that has been built up through, and around, Zionist ideology, and one that places ethno-religious identity above all else, it is clear that the Israeli and Palestinian working classes are not one of the same, simply divided by capitalist exploitation. The importance of acknowledging this is that it is possible to redefine and utilise Marxist concepts in regards to Israel and the occupation of the Palestinian territories. There is no point analysing the conflict and the occupation in its entirety through a Marxist lens – it just cannot work in this case. The occupation, as a complex set of polices built up over decades of control, and tied intrinsically to ideas of national and religious identity and discrimination, has created, however, subset environments, such as the secondary labour market in regards to settlement employment, that can certainly be looked at through the Marxist reserve army of labour lens.

A state-produced reserve army of labour

As previously discussed, Palestinian non-citizen workers in the Israeli labour market have been concentrated in the lower status employment sectors (secondary labour market), such as construction and similar blue collar manual labour work, where wages and job security are minimal compared to the higher-status employment sectors (primary labour market) comprised mainly of Israeli-Jewish citizens. With the implementation of border closure policies on West Bank Palestinian workers by Israel following the outbreak of the *Second Intifada* (see Samara, 2000; Roy, 2001; Hever, 2010) there was a marked reduction in work permits for Palestinians to travel into Israel for employment in the secondary labour market (B'Tselem, 2007). Some of those workers who had their permits terminated and were blacklisted from work in Israel altogether, had even been working with no problems for the same Israeli employer for decades (Kav LaOved, 2012: 22). This reduction in permits was not, however, applied to employment in the settlements. Work in the settlements and work in Israel were, and continue to be, treated differently by the Israeli government when it comes to Palestinian workers. This is true to the extent that even the actual conditions for gaining a permit in the settlements are much more lax than if a worker wishes to gain a permit to work in Israel. For settlement work, an individual has to be 18 or over; for work in Israel, the stipulation is that a worker is at least 22-years-old and has to be married.[1] These conditions for being able to qualify for a work permit in Israel fluctuate frequently, as the age restrictions move up and down depending on the security considerations of the state. The permit age often going up in times of escalation in the conflict, and has been as high as 35 at times since the introduction of the permit regime, while being a parent has also been a stipulation in the past. Crucially, and in contrast to work permits for Israel, the conditions for gaining permits for work in the Israeli settlements have been stagnant for years. In essence, every West Bank Palestinian over the age of 18 in the West Bank is eligible for settlement work. They do not need to be married, and in times of escalation in the conflict, it is uncommon for these conditions to change.[2] Workers that have even been blacklisted from employment in Israel because of security concerns are actually allowed to work in the settlements if they have the authorisation of a local security officer (Kav LaOved, 2012: 37).

Settlement work, therefore, appears to hold a sort of special status in comparison to employment in Israel. Gaining a permit for employment in Israel unlike the settlements is much more unlikely for workers, made even more so with the onset of the *Second Intifada* which saw some employers start the process of replacing Palestinian workers with migrant workers (B'Tselem, 2004, 2007). Settlement work on the other hand has been much less affected by the increased presence of migrant workers.[3] Although Israeli government rhetoric declares the settlements and Israel as one of the same, the permit regime policy clearly shows different. Settlement work permits for West Bank Palestinians are simply much easier to get, as virtually the whole adult population is, in theory, eligible for them. Consequently, Israeli employers in the settlements have a large pool of cheap, easily disposable, and exploitable, West Bank Palestinian workers at their disposal – a much larger pool than Israeli employers in Israel have. It means that with such a high unemployment rate, the hundreds of thousands of unemployed Palestinians are all potential workers for these companies. Yet, in 2016, there were only 27,000 legally employed (permit holding) West Bank Palestinians in the settlements – with an estimated 10,000 or so illegally working. The PGFTU on the other hand claimed during the same time period that there were at least 350,000 unemployed Palestinians in need of work. This gives some indication as to the sheer scale of unemployed workers potentially available to settlement employers and the small number of positions that are in reality available to those workers.

This large employee pool that settlement companies have at their disposal is one that has very limited employment opportunities available to them due to their livelihoods and land being taken from them, a stagnating Palestinian economy, and draconian freedom of movement restrictions that have created precincts of potential employment, all of which have been created by Israeli

state policy. This large pool of unemployed workers has allowed
settler employers to treat employees as disposable, able to fire
and hire workers without consequence, and pay them less than
the legal minimum wage. While this is aided greatly by the Israeli
government which continues to look the other way when it comes
to Palestinian workers' rights, it has also become common practice because employers are aware that the impoverished occupied
workforce have little to no union representation, and that strike
action is virtually impossible as there are so many unemployed
workers desperate for a wage that employees know they can be
easily and quickly replaced.

Settlement employers are therefore exposed to what Karl Marx
conceptualized as a *reserve army of labour*. The relationship is
highly beneficial to employers, and highly exploitative to workers. This reserve army is particularly available to settlement companies over companies based in Israel due to the dynamics of the
precincts of potential employment and the differing conditions
in regards to the permit regime for Israel and for the settlements.
Continued control of the West Bank and the Palestinian economy
by Israeli policymakers through occupation has kept opportunities for Palestinian development and job creation low, and thus
unemployment high, creating a state-manufactured reserve army
of non-citizen Palestinian blue-collar labourers which is used and
exploited by settlement companies for their own benefit. The
benefit is not just limited to the availability of a cheap and pas-
sive workforce, but also the constant availability of more workers gives companies the opportunity to utilise this unemployed
pool when needed depending on production needs. However,
with the Israeli government ultimately having the final say on how
many Palestinian workers are allowed to work in Israel and the

settlements – legally, at least – market forces don't always dictate employer numbers, policy does too. Significantly though, a difference continues to remain between Israel and the settlements. Israeli employers in Israel have pleaded previously to their government to allow for an increase in work permits being issued to meet their production needs, but have been refused – quotas for West Bank Palestinian workers being determined by both the government and the military and set for each industry, for example construction, agriculture and so on (Kav LaOved, 2012: 9). On the other hand, in the settlements and settlement industrial zones, there exists no such quota. While the government and military establishment may still ultimately decide the numbers of workers entering the settlements legally for work, they do not put limits on each employment sector, in theory allowing permit numbers to increase and decrease with much more ease than with which they do for employers in Israel. For example, while construction companies contracted in Israel lament their inability to get their quota increased, construction companies operating in the settlements are, at least in theory, much less limited by such a factor (Ibid: 37). Furthermore the worksite's close proximity to the hometowns of workers means the illegal route for workers is always a potential, although risky, option.

The precincts of potential employment limit which settlements workers can work in, which in effect breaks up this reserve army into smaller constituent parts. The unemployed of Al-Walaja, Nahalin, and Bat'tir, act as a reserve army for nearby settlements such as Ma'ale Adumim, Gilo, and Beitar Illit. Just as unemployed in Al-Jiflik, Al-Fasayall and Az-Zubeidat are for the Jordan Valley agricultural settlements, or Palestinian villages Salfit and Marda are for the large settlement of Ariel that lies deep inside the West

Bank. Up and down the occupied West Bank, there are active and reserve armies of Palestinian labourers, geographically hemmed in, the numbers of both fluctuating up and down depending on the current circumstances. Crucially, there is always a surplus of waiting workers for settlement employers, which doesn't just help with employer's production needs, but also aids in the exploitation of the workforce as a whole.

NINE | State-instigated forced labour

Workers consistently and overwhelmingly claim that having no other choice is the reason behind them working in the Israeli settlements and putting up with the exploitative work conditions that are part and parcel of the settlement employment sector for West Bank Palestinian workers. The work, they say, is not a free choice but a necessity where no other options exist; a way to put food on the table, and scrape a living in the fragile, poverty-stricken, and often dangerous environment of the occupied West Bank. It's not hyperbole. There is no free or genuine choice regarding employment for many workers who have been systematically streamlined into settlement work. Who are, due to circumstances forced on to them, unable to turn down the exploitative and politically damaging settlement work or find any alternative. This idea of no choice has come about due to a combination of several Israeli policies that have purposefully stifled Palestinian development and growth throughout the occupied West Bank, in particular in the rural (read: Area C) communities that have suffered substantially from land annexation. This, coupled with continued, unwavering, and severe freedom of movement restrictions throughout the West Bank, consolidated particularly through the Area A, B, and C system set up originally as part of the Oslo Accords, has created a West Bank consisting of

hundreds of separate and often isolated 'islands' separated by
Israeli checkpoints, roadblocks, settlements, outposts, the Wall,
and settler-only roads, which has, in turn, created separate
precincts of potential employment for West Bank Palestinian
workers (see Chapter 7). Young Palestinian male labourers – who
are the most likely individuals to be employed in settlement work
because of the historical, and state-policy created, funneling of
Palestinian workers into the primary (blue-collar) labour sectors
such as construction and agriculture, industries in which there are
significantly more male workers than female in both Israel and the
Palestinian territories, and which Israeli citizens overwhelmingly
choose not to participate in – are seen by the military establishment as the greatest threats to Israeli security, and subsequently
have, for decades, faced the most draconian freedom of movement restrictions.

As can be seen from the thoughts and words of workers,
because of the economic situation in the West Bank many feel
they have no choice but to be complicit in the construction and
expansion of the illegal settlements, unable to reject such employment because of their (dire and Israeli occupation-created) financial situation and their need to provide for their families. These
workers are heavily exploited, paid less than minimum wage,
their health and safety is routinely compromised by companies
who put profit before safety, and there is no genuine attempt by
the state to enforce the rights of these workers. Fatalities and serious life-altering injuries have occurred because of these conditions, yet many companies prefer to reduce costs by simply not
implementing proper training, equipment, and safe working conditions, in effect putting a (low) price on their workers' health
and lives. Palestinian settlement workers can be fired for minor

misdemeanours, for something that is not their fault, or for no reason at all. Workers feel shame and guilt about their work in the settlements, they face stigma from wider Palestinian society for their role, and through their employment they have become part of their own family's (especially for rural Palestinians whose land has been, and continues to be annexed) and their own nation's, destruction. The work they undertake in the settlements fundamentally helps to create, maintain, and expand the 'facts on the ground' that continue to be the biggest obstacle in the creation of a viable Palestinian state in the West Bank. A reality that is particularly true for Palestinian settlement construction workers whose hands literally build and strengthen the occupation. Workers are well aware of their complicity in the continuation of the current status quo in the West Bank, and the negative consequences that this has for themselves, their family, and the wider Palestinian population. For an estimated 11 percent of settlement workers, there is also the added shame and humiliation of having to work on their family's own stolen land. Considering all of this, it's logical to state then that if other employment options existed or if workers had alternative income streams or savings at their disposal, the vast majority would choose not to work in the settlements. But other options don't exist, including opportunities for self-employment. With Palestinian village land having been taken and annexed by the state of Israel, some families have also lost the opportunity to try and gain some form of food security and self-sufficiency from farming land – possibilities that existed before occupation and to an extent, still did in the early years of occupation when Israel's settlement project was still in its infancy.

Significantly, then, the absence of other employment options for settlement workers is not simply down to other employment options not existing, but rather that other employment options *have purposely not* been allowed to exist because of state policy and state interaction with the West Bank Palestinian blue-collar workforce. West Bank unemployment levels can also be manipulated by Israel depending on security concerns and/or production needs of Israeli capitalists. This is most obviously seen through the permit quotas for travel into Israel for work, as well as permits for work in the settlements which more workers are eligible for and as such ensures, along with the existence of precincts of potential employment, that there will always be a large surplus of workers for settlement companies to dip into when needed. Palestinian development, and therefore potential job creation, can also be encouraged or discouraged through Israeli policies or the strengthening or weakening of Israeli occupation, however the state continues to strangle the Palestinian economy, keeping it dependent on the dominant Israeli one, and starving Palestinians of the opportunity to develop their economy, create jobs, and use their own natural resources. Stuck in precincts of potential employment, and traditional livelihoods stripped from their rural communities, for individuals to reject settlement employment would be to accept poverty.

Fundamentally, then, settlement employment is dictated by an outside force (Israel) with policies that have funneled a vulnerable and asset-stripped population into undesirable employment sectors that the majority of Israeli state citizens do not want to participate in. This workforce is then exploited – in direct disregard to domestic law, but with the backing of the state through the absence and unwillingness of state organs to enforce that law in regards to West Bank Palestinian workers – in order to maximise profit. This, coupled with the reality that the reserve army of labour available to settlement employers has been generated by Israeli policies, shows that this employment is not a free choice for Palestinian settlement workers, but is rather the opposite, and is a nuanced and unique form of state-instigated forced labour by the state of Israel against the occupied and impoverished Palestinian community in rural West Bank areas.

Going against international law?

> Everyone has the right to work, to free choice of employment, to just and favourable conditions of work and to protection against unemployment. (Article 23 (1) United Nations Universal Declaration of Human Rights, 1948)

The overall nature of the employment of Palestinians in the illegal West Bank settlements, with possible notable exception of middlemen, is forced. That is, West Bank Palestinian settlement workers in the vast majority of cases do not have a free choice in their employment. They have been effectively streamlined into the sector through Israeli government policy regarding Palestinian workers, the permit regime, the control of the Palestinian market and economy, and internal freedom of movement restrictions within the West Bank. The choice of not finding other employment options is, therefore, not down simply to other employment options not existing, but as stated previously, rather that other employment options *have purposely not* been allowed to exist.

However, despite this clear forced nature, there are complications that have to be addressed around whether this phenomenon can be regarded as going against international law. The International Labour Organization's 1930 convention on forced labour states that under international law, forced labour shall be defined as "all work or service which is exacted from any person under the menace of any penalty and for which the said person has not offered himself voluntarily" (ILO, 1930). Although the conditions of employment in the settlements for Palestinian workers certainly appear to not be voluntary, and are a direct result of Israeli occupation of Palestinian workers' land and lives, there doesn't necessarily appear at first to be a direct penalty or menace of penalty for not enacting the work. There is one, however: certain poverty. Occupation through the control of Palestinian development, economy and land, and through the creation of precincts of potential employment, has created only one viable route for employment and one possible income stream for rural Palestinian families – settlement work. That route has been built through Israeli occupation and policies, and rejecting settlement work is effectively forcing a worker and their family into financial jeopardy. It is this reality that has led the ILO to state recently that settlement work is not an option for Palestinians employed in the settlements, but rather it is a 'necessity,' in order to survive where there are no other alternative work options and with the looming threat of poverty over their heads (2015: 38).

Within the context of the ILO 1930 definition of forced labour, the organisation has, more recently, ascertained key identifiers in two categories to help determine whether an individual is subjected to forced labour under that 1930 definition. The first category looks at the lack of consent to work, or in other words the actual route into work and how a worker has found themselves in employment and whether that worker has been coerced. The second category looks at whether there is a menace of a penalty for not carrying out the work, or in other words, looks to see what keeps an individual bound to the work, and whether choice exists or not. If a worker's employment fits into at least one identifier in each category, the employment situation can be seen as a case of forced labour.

Under the category of a menace of a penalty, the ILO presents 12 different indicators.[1] At least five of these indicators can be applied in some way to Palestinian settlement workers. There is a threat of *exclusion from future employment* (through blacklisting) if a worker challenges their employer about dangerous work conditions, low wages, lack of worker's rights and so on; this threat also extends to that worker's family who can also be blacklisted from settlement work. Second, as the settlements are covered by Israeli labour law, Palestinian workers are entitled to minimum wage, full legal rights on a par with Israeli-Jewish workers, holiday pay, a pension, and injury compensation. However, settlement employers routinely *remove these rights and/or privileges* and threaten to remove them further or reduce pay if workers complain or speak out about their employment, doing so in the full knowledge that their Palestinian workers feel forced to continue with this employment due to a legitimate feeling of having no choice, or though worry that any complaint will result in being blacklisted. There may also exist the threat of *physical violence* through hired middlemen and security officials or *denunciation to authorities* if a worker complains or speaks out about aspects of their employment. These four indicators, however, do not necessarily bond a worker into the employment, although they do ensure that the employment situation will not and does not improve, and exploitation continues. It is the fifth indicator of *financial penalties* that really ties settlement work to the concept of forced labour and specifically the idea of state-forced labour. The first four indicators exist, but in regards to ensuring the working conditions remain exploitative, dangerous, and the vast majority of workers remain underpaid – and therefore significantly, cannot build up a bank of savings that could help them move away from settlement work in the future. It is, however, the threat of crippling poverty which Israel has subjected many rural Palestinian communities to, especially those that sit beside settlements and have had much of their land taken from them, that forces workers into the settlement sector and keeps them there despite their exploitation. If a worker refuses employment in the settlements, they are effectively plunging themselves and their family into certain financial peril.

Under the ILO's category regarding the route into forced labour, of which nine indicators are given,[2] it is possible to look at Palestinian settlement workers under the indicator given of *physical confinement in the work location*. This is contentious, as the ILO specifically mentions prison or private detention within this. The unique political situation of the West Bank and Israeli occupation, however, poses questions to this rather narrow interpretation. Israeli occupation, and the division of the West Bank into separate zones, further divided up by checkpoints, roadblocks, the Wall, settlements, and settler-only roads, has created a series of smaller areas, or bantustans, within the West Bank that many Palestinians are restricted to. Settlement workers are, as such, confined to *precincts of potential employment*. There is scope, therefore, to state that many Palestinian settlement workers *are* indeed physically confined in and around their work location, which is a state-created situation that has forced them into the only form of employment openly available to them – settlement work – a form that ripped their land and livelihoods from them when it appeared unwanted, and illegally on their doorsteps. Consequently workers are effectively rooted to where they live and the nearby surrounding area; their freedom of movement, like that of many Palestinians, particularly young males, is severely restricted. The International Trade Union Confederation (ITUC) states that forced labour in an illegal context can result from restrictions to movement, such as the inability to move from town to town through formal (read: state-instigated) procedures (2008: 13). Anti-slavery, an organisation that attempts to highlight and combat cases of forced labour around the world, also states that victims of forced labour "are frequently from minority or marginalised groups who face institutionalised discrimination" that can be forced into particular employment due to "restricting their freedom of movement" (2013). If we accept the notion that it is the settlement companies that exploit and use workers, but fundamentally it is the state that has created these precincts of potential employment and given Palestinian settlement workers no choice but to work in these settlements and forced them into these exploitative circumstances, then it appears that settlement workers are subject to forced labour under the ILO's definition. The work is not a free choice, and cannot be seen as voluntary for the vast majority of workers because of the circumstances they live in – which are dictated from above by a powerful government with an often heavy handed and deadly military. Furthermore, by carrying out settlement work, these workers actually bolster the settlements and depressingly add to their own dire situation and further bond themselves into settlement employment.

Moreover, if we strip back our notion of forced labour, it is possible to see where and how settlement work fits into the concept further. The idea of forced labour brings up, for understandable historical and logical reasons, the idea of this concept being completely negative in every aspect. First, the idea that something is forced, means the person/persons/group involved has had no choice but to undertake the work. This is an airtight fact. It cannot be disputed. Forced labour is exactly that: forced. What constitutes forced is, however, more flexible. 'Forced' can mean enslavement, abduction, threat of punishment, or in the examples given above, being confined and restricted within a space, area, or building, among other things. The second idea that forced labour logically brings up, is that whatever the worker has been forced into, is something that is negative for them, that is, it is something they do not want to do. This makes sense, but only because this is how situations of forced labour generally play out. Forced labour, hypothetically, despite not being a free choice and involving the menace or threat of a penalty, need not be completely negative to the individual who is in the forced work. As an illustrative example, let's take an individual, let's call them A, who is hemmed into a geographical area by outside forces (a government for example, or other institution), and cannot leave, move away, or come and go by free will. The only way A can ensure they do not starve is to earn money to buy food. The outside force does not allow A to farm the land they stand on, or use any of the natural resources around them. This is the reality A lives in, they can't produce food for themself; they're not allowed. The outside force has a business however, which also happens to be the only form of employment in the area A is hemmed into – it's the only business that is allowed. A must work there to put food on their table and to look after their family. The business can treat A as they like, they may withhold their wages, threaten them with physical violence or dismissal, they may pay them terribly or not at all, and make them work long hours in dangerous conditions.

But in this case the business actually pays a decent wage to A, and in a stroke of luck actually carries out work, *Work Z*, that A enjoys. *Work Z* just happens to be A's dream job. Something they enjoy, that gives them pleasure, a feeling of self-worth, and a job that they have wanted to do their whole life. None of this however fundamentally stops *Work Z* from being forced labour. The work is not a free choice; it has still been forced on A in order to survive. The power relationship remains the same; the outside force dictates where A must work and what they must do in order to survive. Even if A is happy about the work, that does not mean that A is now in control, because they are not. Even if A is being paid well for the work, and is not being exploited, the power relationship still stays the same – there continues to be no free choice made, and the forced dynamic of the relationship still rules over anything else. The way forced labour can work then, if you look at this case, is that the actual labour aspect of it does not need to be this concept of something horrific, such as slave labour, and it can hypothetically be a very well-paid job, as well as a very badly paid or non-waged job. Exploitation of the worker does not need to be a rule, but it is hard to imagine a case where it never will be. The importance of this understanding is that settlement companies and Israeli government officials often espouse rhetoric claiming that the settlements are a good thing because they provide work for Palestinians. Although Palestinian settlement workers overwhelmingly say they hate the work, are exploited and paid illegal wages, feel shame from it, and that it's their only choice and they must undertake the work as a matter of necessity, it is not unknown to find a settlement worker who is thankful for the work, or settlement employment that, although still exploitative and paying below the Israeli minimum wage, may pay more than what a worker may get if working in a similar job in a Palestinian Authority area.

Crucially, none of this changes the forced nature of the employment, or the power dynamics of that employment and the historical and current roots to its existence. The inherent nature of the work remains forced. Similar lines of defence used by settlement companies – that they provide employment to an impoverished population who should be thankful for any work that comes their way – has also been made by sweatshops in the past to try and legitimise the exploitation of its workers (Heintz, 2006). Illegitimate businesses such as sweatshops, as well as businesses working in the illegal Israeli settlements, are both operating with the primary purpose to exploit a desperate and vulnerable workforce for cheap production. Joint Israeli-Palestinian research center *Who Profits* aptly described this spurious defence by settlement companies as "blatant attempts to distract public attention from the Israeli occupation and the daily hardships suffered by Palestinians, who are compelled to seek their livelihoods in Israeli industries" (2012: 1). A business that pursues lower production costs at the expense of a workforce that is forced into the exploitative workplace conditions in order to survive cannot demand legitimacy because of the existence of that workforce, while specifically creating an environment at that workforce's expense. An environment that is focused around workforce exploitation, and that benefits from that workforce's continued loss or land, livelihood, and self-determination aspirations.

Another important illustrative example of how the nature of settlement employment can be inherently forced is by looking at forced transfer (deportation) in the occupied Palestinian territories. Forced transfer or displacement brings up images of armed soldiers or militia members, guns cocked, forcibly loading people onto lorries and physically transporting them against their will to another place. This is forced transfer, but so is the "involuntary or induced movement of people resulting from the creation of insecurity, disorder, or other adverse conditions, for the purpose of, or resulting in such migration" (Melon, 2012: 28). The International Criminal Tribunal for the former Yugoslavia (ICTY) appeals chamber has also stated previously during court proceedings that forced transfer should not and cannot be just limited to the idea of physical force violently deporting groups of people, and that "factors other than force itself may render an act involuntary" (2006).[3] What can be deduced and what has been continually ratified in regards to what does and does not constitute forced transfer, is whether the displacement taking place is the choice of the people being displaced or not. In the context of the occupied West Bank, it has been widely documented that Israeli policies contribute to creating a situation of forced transfer for some Palestinians, especially for those living in rural Area C communities, where, due to unbearable living conditions, and being deprived of their livelihood and ability to move due to severe freedom of movement restrictions, some feel forced to leave their homes and land (Ibid: 32). Just as Israeli occupation has displaced Palestinian families and communities in the West Bank, forcing them to move elsewhere to survive, so it has forced families and communities into the settlement employment sector – the choice to carry out or not carry out the work for many settlement workers, as they repeatedly claim, does not exist. Just as occupation and the occupation structure has created – and is implicit in – the forced displacement of Palestinians in the West Bank, it has created – and is implicit in – the forced labour in the settlements.

State-instigated forced labour

Certainly the phenomenon of Palestinians working in, and building, the illegal Israeli settlements in the West Bank appears at
first to be a contradictory one. Through an analysis of the Israeli
state's interactions with Palestinian settlement workers, and
Palestinian blue collar workers in general, however, it is possible
to dissect the layers that have led to this apparent contradiction
taking place. Through the segregated labour market whereby
Palestinian non-citizen workers from the West Bank were placed
below Israeli-Jewish citizens as secondary workers in the Israeli
labour market, coupled with continued occupation of the Palestinian territories that stifles any prospect of economic progress, a
dependency for those Palestinians on labouring jobs within Israel
and the settlements was created.

Workers feel they have no choice but to work in the settlement
employment sector, having been funneled into this employment
through a stagnating Palestinian economy that is unable to produce
employment opportunities for these workers due to Israeli occupation and economic policies, and continued freedom of movement restrictions internally in the West Bank that have created
precincts of potential employment. The idea that these workers are
trapped within this form of employment is furthered by the apparent shame they feel for this work and the unwillingness they often
have in talking about it. If a choice existed and/or if a worker could
afford economically not to be employed within this sector, they
would not take up employment considering the shame felt, as well
as the dangerous work conditions, low wages, lack of legal rights,
and potential threatening behaviour that could be experienced
within the work environment. Crucially, while settlement businesses benefit from this – through a cheap, disposable workforce

and the existence of reserve armies of Palestinian labourers – it is not those employers who have created the forced nature of the circumstances for workers, but is instead the state. The International Labor Organization definition of forced labour under international law is narrow when applied to this circumstance, yet considering the completely unique situation regarding Israeli occupation of the West Bank and the consequences of the settlements on the rural Palestinian population, there does exist the potential for this use (or misuse) of Palestinian workers in the settlements (as state-projects) to fall under the remit of international law. It is not unreasonable to state, therefore, that the role of freedom of movement restrictions in the West Bank, and the occupation's control of land, life, and livelihoods has left workers with no choice but to take up the damaging (politically and socially) low-waged and sometimes hazardous employment within state-sponsored projects – the settlements – through companies that often reject those workers' legal rights, who are able to hire and fire at ease because of a state-created reserve army of labour, with the state happily looking the other way. Settlement work can be seen, and is, a new and subtle form of state-instigated forced labour, that the government of Israel must acknowledge, address, and answer for.

Notes

ONE

1. Interview with Mahmoud, labourer, 26 January 2016.
2. Using a conversion rate of 1 USD (United States Dollar) to 3.8 NIS (New Israeli Shekel).
3. The 25 NIS Israeli minimum wage was implemented in April 2015, the daily minimum wage for a full-time employee working five days a week, however, is 214.62 NIS, and for an employee working six days a week, 186 NIS. This does not include overtime. (National Insurance Institute of Israel, 2015)
4. See High Court of Justice (HCJ) ruling HCJ 5666/03, *Kav LaOved et al. v. National Labor Court in Jerusalem et al.*
5. Interview with Abed Dari, Kav LaOved fieldworker working with Palestinian workers employed in the Israeli settlements, 3 May 2016. Also see Sbeih's study (2011), which found that 88 percent of Palestinians employed in the settlements on a monthly basis were being paid less than minimum wage.
6. Interview with Mousa, labourer, 7 May 2016.
7. Interview with Khader, labourer, 7 May 2016.
8. It is worth noting that a concrete wall only comprises roughly ten percent of the overall length of the Wall. The remaining 90 percent is made up of a combination of barbed wire fences, military towers and roads, and no-go firing zones that can at times be hundreds of meters wide.
9. Interview with Ibrahim, construction worker, 7 May 2016.
10. Land annexation by Israel has come in many different forms. Land may be seized as nature reserves, or for military means and military use (although much of the initial land annexed by the military was then

turned over for civilian use to create and expand the settlements), or through the state declaring land, 'state land,' through using an aggressive interpretation of Ottoman Law where land becomes the property of the state if it is not cultivated for three consecutive years. Israel has annexed over 1.3 million dunams (130,000 hectares) using this tactic, of which only 0.7 percent has been allocated for Palestinian use (Levinson, 2013).

11. The Allon plan guided Israeli policy in the immediate aftermath of the 1967 occupation of the West Bank, which sought to annex Palestinian land and establish the first settlements in the Hebron Hills, Jordan Valley, and Gush Etzion.

12. See Weizmann's (2007) study on the architecture of occupation.

13. The State of Israel argued that the Wall was built with security in mind. Israeli human rights NGO B'Tselem however discovered through analysing the route that the Wall takes, that its path actually corresponds with plans that were already in place in regards to the expansion of the settlements (B'Tselem, 2005: 12).

14. Having a permit to work in a settlement grants that individual the permission only to enter, work, and leave that settlement. It does not grant permission to travel to Israel, or enter Jerusalem, for example.

15. See for example interview with Anwar Rabutim, Al-Walaja Village Council, 23 January 2016: "A lot of people in this village have lost land because of Israel, people have lost jobs, they used to farm, do agriculture. It wasn't much money, but it was a steady job. But when the land was lost, they didn't have a choice, they had to go and work in the settlements around here, doing construction, building, it's the only job they can get."

16. Interview with Mohammed, handyman, 26 January 2016.

17. Known participation in the Israeli labour market for Hebron stands at 5 percent (ARIJ, 2009); Bethlehem 3 percent (ARIJ, 2010b); Nablus 3 percent (ARIJ, 2014a). In comparison to, for example Al-Walaja, 47 percent (ARIJ, 2010a); Majdal Bani Fadil, 60 percent (ARIJ, 2014b); Nahalin, 40 percent (ARIJ, 2010c).

18. Interview with Fadi, labourer, 26 January 2016.

19. Interview with Aymad, electrician, 23 January 2016.

20. Interview with Khader, labourer, 7 May 2016.

21. Under the terms of the Oslo Accords, Area A comprises around 18 percent of the West Bank and is under PA civil and security authority,

although Israeli army incursions into Area A are frequent. Area B comprises around 22 percent, and is under PA civil control, but complete Israeli security control. Area C is under complete Israeli control.

TWO

1. Interview with Abed, middleman, 26 January 2016.
2. Interview with Hashem Masarrwa, Palestinian lawyer working with Palestinian settlement workers, 6 February 2016. See also Human Rights Watch, 2016: 96.
3. With virtually no attempt by employers or Israeli authorities to educate Palestinian workers of their rights, or even translate relevant documents, the vast majority of workers have no idea of what they are entitled to, or that a minimum wage even exists. (B'Tselem, 2010; Kav LaOved, 2012).
4. Records of employee hours and payment have to be submitted to Israel's Payment Division, which operates under the Ministry of the Interior.
5. Interview with Hussain Foqha, PGFTU Director, 6 January 2016.
6. See Wage Protection Law (Amendment 24) 5768-2008, Sec 26(b).
7. The 2007 High Court of Justice ruling rejected the idea that the middleman could also be an employer, which would have given a level of legal protection to employers using them to exploit their workers. Despite this, Human Rights Watch has discovered at least one case since that HCJ ruling, where a lower Israeli court has accepted a company's claim that the middleman was also the employer (Human Rights Watch, 2016: 89).
8. Interview with Qassem, middleman, 9 May 2016.
9. Interview with Abed, middleman, 26 January 2016. Interview with Qassem, middleman, 9 May 2016. See also B'Tselem, 2010; Sbeih, 2011; Kav LaOved, 2012.
10. Fees can crop up almost anywhere, and are seemingly often just created by employers to try and siphon more of a worker's wage away from them. Sbeih (2011) recorded that 13 percent of settlement workers were even being forced to pay fees to their employers to pay for hired Israeli guards who would guard the workers while on worksites.
11. Thai migrant workers make up 95 percent of the agricultural workforce in Israel, they are often paid less than minimum wage, and

suffer labour abuses against them (see Khalel, Vickery, 2015; Vickery, 2016a) albeit not usually to the extent that Palestinian settlement workers do. With another cheap workforce competing for employment in the agricultural settlements, Palestinian workers find themselves working for cheaper than migrant workers in order to get jobs. Wages for a day's work for Palestinian workers can be as little as 60 NIS (see Chapter 3).

12. Interview with Mousa, chef, 23 January 2016.

THREE

1. Interview with Yazan, agricultural worker, 11 February 2016.
2. See Youth Employment Law 1953.
3. Interview with Abu Fuad, Mukhtar of Fasayll, 11 February 2016.
4. This decrease in population can be seen as a form of forced population transfer, as Israeli policies and occupation have been geared towards moving Israeli settlers into the Jordan Valley by providing favourable conditions (land, water, financial incentives) for them, while on the other hand making life increasingly difficult or impossible for Palestinians (land grabs, lack of water availability, Israeli control of economy, freedom of movement restrictions) living in the valley. See Melon (2012) for a detailed account on forcible transfer of the Jordan Valley Palestinian population since 1967.
5. Interview with Mohammed, agricultural worker, 11 February 2016.
6. Interview with Laith, agricultural worker, 11 February 2016.
7. Interview with Jamela, agricultural worker, 24 February 2016.
8. One notable exception exists. Unauthorised construction and building by settlers and settlements in Area C is often authorised retroactively (Halper, Schaeffer, 2012).
9. Interview with Zacharia, agricultural worker, 24 February 2016.
10. Interview with Mohammed, agricultural worker, 24 February 2016.
11. Sbeih's study (2011) of 485 Palestinian settlement workers found that 58 percent of agricultural workers were working 12-14 hour days.
12. Interview with Shaul, Israeli farmer in Tomer settlement, 3 March 2016. Shaul had been confirmed by members of Fasayll and Palestinian settlement workers as an employer who employs children on his farm. He denied the charges.

55

FOUR

1. Interview with Faiza, agricultural worker, 25 February 2016.
2. The legal minimum daily wage is 214.62 NIS for a full time worker, working five days a week.
3. Interview with Fuzaylah, agricultural worker, 25 February 2016.
4. Interview with Aymad, electrician, 23 January 2016.
5. Since 2013, UNRWA has been supporting approximately 300,000 Palestinians from 70,000 families, with basic food commodities (UNRWA, 2016).
6. Interview with Hakim [name changed], construction worker, 27 January 2016.
7. See for example, Kav LaOved (2012); Human Rights Watch (2016).
8. Group interview with injured Palestinian settlement workers, Jericho, 6 February 2016.
9. Interview with Ahmad, construction worker, 6 February 2016.
10. Interview with Abed Dari, Kav LaOved fieldworker working with Palestinian workers employed in the Israeli settlements, 6 February 2016.
11. Interview with Taghrid Shbita, Kav LaOved fieldworker working with Palestinian workers employed in the Israeli settlements, 8 August 2013.
12. This idea has been expressed by PA officials who, even though aware that the PA cannot provide alternative jobs, and have some general sympathy towards the plight of settlement workers, see construction work as generally inexcusable. For example, the Mayor of Qabatiya, Ali Zakarni, admitted in a 2013 interview with the author that he did not mind workers doing agricultural work for the settlements, but that "the construction of the buildings, it's really bad."
13. Interview with Hamza, garage owner, 23 January 2016.
14. Interview with Hussain Foqha, PGFTU Director, 6 January 2016.
15. See Weizmann's (2007) excellent study on the architecture of occupation, and how Israel has moulded the West Bank and its infrastructure in a way to ensure complete control.

FIVE

1. Sa'ir, a poverty-stricken village heavily impacted by Israel's closure policies in the West Bank, became a hotbed of attempted (some confirmed, some alleged) stabbing attacks against Israeli soldiers by villagers during

the 2015–16 escalation in violence in Israel and Palestine, coined as the *Knife Intifada*, due to the number of incidents involving Palestinian knife attacks. See Vickery (2016b).

2. Interview with Mohammed, construction worker, 12 January 2016.

3. Interview with Mahmoud, construction worker, 26 January 2016.

4. Despite them ignoring and refusing to implement domestic labour law, according to the United Nations Guiding Principles on Business and Human Rights, companies have a responsibility to adhere to and respect domestic labour law along with the rights listed by the International Labour's Declaration on Fundamental Principles and Rights at Work. Discrimination due to ethnicity or nationality is included within this.

5. Interview with Oron Meiri, Israeli lawyer representing Palestinian workers in Israel's High Court of Justice (HCJ), 7 January 2016.

6. Ministerial Committee for Security Affairs, Resolution No. B/1, 1970.

7. Employment of Workers in Certain Locations (Judea and Samaria) No. 967. 5742-1982.

8. Interview with Abed Dari, Kav LaOved fieldworker working with Palestinian workers employed in the Israeli settlements, 6 February 2016.

9. Interview with Hashem Masarrwa, Palestinian lawyer working with Palestinian settlement workers, 6 February 2016.

10. Interview with Oron Meiri, Israeli lawyer representing Palestinian workers in Israel's High Court of Justice (HCJ), 7 January 2016.

11. Interview with Mohammed, agricultural worker, 24 February 2016. Interview with Zacharia, agricultural worker, 24 February 2016.

12. Written contracts for Palestinian workers in the Israeli labour market in general (Israel and the settlements) are very rare (Bank of Israel, 2015).

13. See High Court of Justice (HCJ) ruling HCJ 5666/03, *Kav LaOved et al. v. National Labor Court in Jerusalem et al.*

14. Interview with Hashem Masarrwa, Palestinian lawyer working with Palestinian settlement workers, 6 February 2016.

15. Interview with Ibrahim, construction worker, 7 May 2016.

16. Committee for Public Inquiry, Protocol No. 28, 2013.

17. Interview with Oron Meiri, Israeli lawyer representing Palestinian workers in Israel's High Court of Justice (HCJ), 7 January 2016. Interview with Hashem Masarrwa, Palestinian lawyer working with Palestinian settlement workers, 6 February 2016.

18. 97,000 Palestinians from the occupied West Bank, and Gaza Strip, were treated in Israeli hospitals in 2015 due to PA medical facilities being unable to perform certain procedures. Author correspondence with the Coordinator of Government Activities in the Territories (COGAT), 10 May 2016.

19. Group interview with injured Palestinian settlement workers, Jericho, 6 February 2016.

20. Interview with Mohammed, factory worker, Jericho, 6 February 2016.

21. See for example: Hachlili (2015).

22. One worker even remarked that he believed that despite the ban, the PA were secretly happy with settlement workers as they have been forced to "manage our own situation, and this means they [PA] don't have to look for alternatives for us." Interview with Mousa, labourer, 7 May 2016.

23. Interview with Hussain Foqha, PGFTU Director, 6 January 2016.

24. Interview with Taghrid Shbita, Kav LaOved fieldworker working with Palestinian workers employed in the Israeli settlements, 8 August 2013.

SIX

1. With the notable exception of the Druze community in Israel, an ethnic community that at times self-identifies as Palestinian. Druze leaders signed the "blood covenant," in 1956 with Israeli leaders, to set in motion the compulsory conscription of Druze youth. See Firro (1999) for more background on the Druze in Israel and the community's relationship to compulsory conscription.

2. See, for example, Ben White's excellent book *Palestinians in Israel: Segregation, Discrimination and Democracy* (2011), which shows comprehensively the discrimination that Palestinian citizens of Israel face in the country, including vis-à-vis their employment and employment options.

3. It was in the aftermath of the 1991 Gulf War that there was a shift in policy towards Palestinian workers entering Israel. Previously the labour force could move relatively freely unless an individual had been blacklisted. That shift however began to require non-citizen Palestinian workers to be in possession of a work permit (Arnon, Spivak, 1998).

4. Israel's closure policy, which in essence is the swift clamping down on border movements by Israel when the state claims to have security concerns regarding the Palestinian population (for example during an escalation in conflict), virtually closes off the West Bank from Israel and/or the settlements, shores up borders, increases roadblocks and checkpoints, and denies entry to permit-holding Palestinians. Policies of closure can apply to the Palestinian population as a whole, but also can be imposed on certain groups, for example age, sex, village/town/ city residing in, and so on. Closure could close off the Palestinian population from the Israeli one completely, but also IDF soldiers may also close a Palestinian city off from its surroundings for example, stopping the movement in and out of the center for a specified period of time. These policies of closure have been described as a form of collective punishment in the past due to their sweeping nature against all Palestinians, or all Palestinians of a certain age, area, sex etc. See, for example: Human Rights Watch (1996), Cohen (2016), and Dearden (2016).

5. For example there was a willingness by Israel to offer a Free Trade Agreement to Gaza but nothing of the sort to the West Bank, while at the same time clamping down on Gaza border breaches in the years following in an effort to end illegal workers crossing – despite continued demand for cheap Gazan workers – something that was never done with the West Bank (Farsakh, 2002: 21).

6. Although there was some effect on West Bank Palestinian worker numbers in Israel, certainly with the onset of the *Second Intifada*, as some Israeli employers made an effort to replace their Palestinian workforce with a migrant workforce (see for example: Ellman and Laacher, 2003).

7. It is worth noting, however, that there exists a social hierarchy within the Israeli-Jewish community of Israel, which in general places Ashkenazi Jews (who are of Eastern European origin) at the top, followed by Sephardic Jews (whose descendants are from the Mediterranean areas), with Mizrahi Jews (of Arab origin) at the bottom. This has led there to be, for example, a large wage gap between Ashkenazim and Mizrahim (Rettig Gur, 2014). An Israeli-Jewish citizen of Arab descent (Mizrahim) may also therefore hold a similar job, or economic status as a Palestinian–Israeli citizen of the state, yet the fact that the latter is not Jewish within the context of Israel, places that citizen below the former due to

a higher social capital, which can lead to better employment, wage, etc. Carrying out military duty also carries significant social benefits.

8. A good example of the fluctuating supply and demand needs of Israeli employers are construction companies working in the settlements where projects are often dictated by Israeli government policy regarding the expansion of settlements and creation of new settlement housing units (see for example: Levinson, Lis, Ravid, 2013; Ravid, 2015).

9. *Eretz Israel* is the concept of greater Israel, that is, an Israel that encompasses both the land of the current state of Israel *and* the Palestinian territories. Though there have also been claims that *Eretz Israel* also incorporates parts of Jordan.

10. The Paris Protocol was actually intended as a five-year interim economic agreement, but continues to dictate and control economic policy more than two decades later.

11. Although it is worth noting that the currency had been effectively forced on the occupied Palestinian territories since the very beginning of the occupation.

12. Despite Israeli complaints, this move was eventually successful with the Palestinian Authority becoming a formal member on the 1st April 2015.

13. These revenues coming from, for example, taxes on Palestinian exports. It's noteworthy that in regards to Palestinian exports, along with Israel controlling what reaches the market, and in what quantities, the state also takes a cut of 3 percent of the revenues (as dictated by the Paris Protocol) as a fee for collecting on behalf of the Palestinian Authority (see Palestine Ministry of Finance, 2014).

14. Except with the notable exception of the Gaza Strip's southern border with Egypt, where there is a large illicit smuggling business of goods and materials through an extensive number of tunnels that are buried underneath the Egypt-Gaza border. Although, it's worth nothing that these tunnels are frequently destroyed by either Egyptian authorities, or the Israeli air force, so there is no permanent and stable tunnel economy as such.

15. Even the items Israel chooses to allow out of the West Bank in order to export to outside markets, for example Palestinian agricultural produce, is often subjected to lengthy delays as producers are not allowed to take the product directly out of the West Bank, but rather it must be

offloaded at the Israeli checkpoint, searched, go through lengthy security checks and protocols before being reloaded again. This process, called *back-to-back transfers*, is not required for products entering the West Bank – i.e. Israeli products. The World Bank has commented on this process previously, stating that along with the delays that come from this process – costing time and money – back-to-back transfers "also result in substantial damage to goods when they are cross loaded or manually inspected" (World Bank, 2008: ii). Back-to-back transfers are one example of many Israeli policy-driven barriers to Palestinian trade, both physical and bureaucratic, that aim to impede the creation of a functioning Palestinian West Bank economy.

16. For an idea of how significant an injection of this amount of money would be, the revenues created from tax to the Palestinian Authority from this, would wipe out half the organisation's debt in one year (Human Rights Watch, 2016: 10).

17. Regarding the raw materials coming from Israeli quarries in the occupied West Bank, 94 percent of those materials are going to the Israeli market (Human Rights Watch, 2016: 43). The benefits don't just stretch to the economic aspects of this. People, in general, don't like the idea of having large mining and quarrying activities, or industrial sites and factories, beside where they live – for Israelis those eye-sore industries have conveniently been moved out of their sight, and are located in the settlements beside Palestinian communities, rather than beside Israeli ones.

18. Resources extracted by the occupying power can only be used for the needs of the occupied population. According to international law, "the occupying power can only dispose of the resources of the occupied territory to the extent necessary for the current administration of the territory and to meet the essential needs of the population" (Institut de Droit International, 2003). See also Benvenisti, 2012: 82.

19. A select list of benefits for individual settlers include the ability to buy housing with a government-subsidised mortgage, free school transportation, higher salaries for teachers, and free education from the age of three upwards. For industry, taxes are much cheaper in the settlements than over the Green Line in Israel, there are significant grants and subsidies available that are not available to companies within Israel, while there is also reimbursement of taxes from products exported to

the European Union. A full list of the communities that come under National Priority status can be obtained from Israel's Ministry of Construction.

20. For example exports from the settlements to Israel's largest trade partner, the European Union, comes to $300 million a year. This is a conservative estimate. While settlement farms export more of their produce (66 percent) outside of Israel than any other region inside the country (Human Rights Watch, 2016: 101).

SEVEN

1. Corruption exists in the Palestinian Authority and has been known about for years (see Samara, 2000). If the PA had more money at its disposal from being able to generate revenue from natural resources and development, there is no guarantee that money would be exempt from practices of corruption also. Although it is reasonable to believe that if occupation did not exist, the PA would not exist in its current form. That is a form that relies heavily on outside funds, is used by the Israeli government to help control the Palestinian population, and where corruption is accepted and not challenged in order to help keep the political class in power and control – the political status quo of the PA elites remaining in power being favourable to Israel. For just one example of many available, see the so-called 'Palestine Papers' (Palestine Papers, 2011), leaked documents that were released by Al Jazeera in 2011 that showed the security co-operation between Israel and PA authorities, and that even discussed potential assassinations of high-profile Palestinian figures (Khoury, Issacharoff et al., 2011).

2. Correct as of May 2015 (B'Tselem, 2015).

3. See the deaths of 17-year-old Adnan Ayed Hamed Mashni, or 36-year old Ahmad Riyad Mahmoud Shehadeh as a couple of examples (B'Tselem, 2016).

4. In the rare cases where the severity decreases, however, this is temporary and due to an attempt to diffuse rising tensions at the occupation in the West Bank, rather than allowing the Palestinian economy or general situation to improve in the long term (LO, 2015: 20).

5. The International Court of Justice (ICJ), the United Nations primary judicial organ, issued an advisory opinion on 9th July 2004 stating that

the construction of the Wall should be ceased and completed parts of the Wall taken down. Although the advisory committee recognised that Israel 'has the right, and indeed the duty, to respond in order to protect the life of its citizens, the committee explicitly noted that "the measures taken are bound nonetheless to remain in conformity with applicable international law" (ICJ, 2004: 12). However, the Wall's construction and current deviating path, which adversely affects Palestinians, has violated Israel's obligations under international law. The ICJ also stated that Israel should pay all reparations for the "requisition and destruction of homes, businesses and agricultural holdings" and "return the land, orchards, olive groves, and other immovable property seized" (Ibid: 14). A sentiment also overwhelmingly approved by the United Nations General Assembly on 20th July 2004 in Resolution ES-10/15, which stipulated that Israel must comply with the ICJ ruling.

6. The Wall's structure itself comprises 61 kilometers of concrete wall up to nine meters high in some of the Palestinian built-up areas – which sometimes literally splits towns, cities, and families in half. The rest is made up mainly of a 15 foot electric fence, surrounded by 135–300 foot wide 'security zones,' barbed wire, intrusion-detection pathways, Israeli army military roads and anti-vehicle ditches. Although less than 10 percent of the Wall is actually concrete walling, the fenced areas that can be hundreds of meters wide and heavily guarded, are often more impenetrable than the actual walled parts.

7. Israeli human rights NGO B'Tselem discovered through analysing the route that the Wall takes, that its path actually corresponds with plans that were already in place in regards to the expansion of the settlements (2005: 12). The Wall, rather than having security as the reason for conception, has instead had land annexation and control of the Palestinian population as its core *raison d'être*.

8. Outposts are unauthorised settlements set up by radical Israeli settlers who, in their quest for *Eretz Israel* and to further break up Palestinian communities in the West Bank, look to increase the settler presence in the occupied West Bank through setting up new settlements on land, particularly hilltops, not currently occupied by settlers. These outposts, which often begin as a single cabin, a few tents or caravans, are illegal under Israeli law. In spite of this, once set up, they often receive

government backing, support and IDF protection, and as they increase in size over the years, they are often given legal status under Israeli law, being classed as an extension of previous settlements or declared as new ones completely. This retroactive legalisation of outposts continues to actively encourage the creation of new outposts in the West Bank (The Rights Forum and Yesh Din, 2015; Peace Now, 2015).

9. See, for example, the Israeli government's own Sason Report (2005), *Summary of the Opinion Concerning Unauthorized Outposts*, which looks at how outposts are initially added to already existing infrastructure

10. Known participation in the Israeli labour market, for example, includes: Hebron 5 percent (ARIJ, 2009); Bethlehem 3 percent (ARIJ, 2010b); Nablus 3 percent (ARIJ, 2014a). Rural Palestinian villages that are situated near the settlements have much higher percentage figures, such as: Al-Walaja, 47 percent (ARIJ, 2010a); Majdal Bani Fadil, 60 percent (ARIJ, 2014b); Nahalin, 40 percent (ARIJ, 2010c).

11. This, of course, isn't a problem just restricted to communities in the Jordan Valley. Marda, a Palestinian village of under 2,000 in the central West Bank had its herding- and farming-based economy destroyed by loss of land to the nearby Ariel settlement and the Wall. The village used to have around 10,000 animals, that number has dropped to 100 (Human Rights Watch, 2016: 73).

EIGHT

1. Correct as of May 2016. Author correspondence with Israel's Coordinator of Government Activities (COGAT).

2. Though it is worth noting that the Israeli military does sometimes implement closure policies on these workers, for example not allowing workers to enter the settlements for a day or a few days following a Palestinian attack or a string of attacks on soldiers or settlers. Such a closure for settlement workers is, however, relatively rare, and when it does happen, very short in length.

3. Although in the agricultural sector there are Thai workers working alongside West Bank Palestinian workers, as part of a bilateral agreement to attract Thai agricultural workers to Israel signed by both the Israeli and Thai governments (Vickery, 2016a).

NINE

1. Which arc: physical violence against a worker or family or close associates; sexual violence; (threat of) supernatural retaliation; imprisonment or other physical confinement; financial penalties; denunciation to authorities (police, immigration, and so on) and deportation; exclusion from future employment; exclusion from community and social life; removal of rights or privileges; deprivation of food, shelter, or other necessities; shift to even worse working conditions; loss of social status (International Labor Organization, 2008: 9).

2. Which are: birth/descent into 'slave' or bonded status; physical abduction or kidnapping; sale of person into the ownership or another; physical confinement in the work location; psychological compulsion, i.e. an order to work, backed up by a credible threat of a penalty for non-compliance; induced indebtedness; deception of false promises about types and terms of work; withholding and non-payment of wages; retention of identity documents or other valuable personal possessions (International Labor Organization, 2008: 9).

3. The Prosecutor v. Milomir Stakić. IT-97-24-T, Appeals Chamber, Judgment, 22 (2006).

Bibliography

Alenat, S. (2010) 'Palestinian Workers in the West Bank Settlements', *Kav LaOved*.

Applied Research Institute – Jerusalem. (2009) 'Hebron City Profile', *Applied Research Institute – Jerusalem*.

Applied Research Institute – Jerusalem. (2010a) 'Al Walaja Village Profile', *Applied Research Institute – Jerusalem*.

Applied Research Institute – Jerusalem. (2010b) 'Bethlehem City Profile', *Applied Research Institute – Jerusalem*.

Applied Research Institute – Jerusalem. (2010c) 'Nahalin Village Profile', *Applied Research Institute – Jerusalem*.

Applied Research Institute – Jerusalem. (2014a) 'Nablus City Profile', *Applied Research Institute – Jerusalem*.

Applied Research Institute – Jerusalem. (2014b) 'Majdal Bani Fadil Village Profile', *Applied Research Institute – Jerusalem*.

Anti-Slavery. (2013) 'What is Forced Labour?', *Anti-Slavery*.

Arnon, A. and Spivak, A. (1998) 'Economic Aspects of the Oslo Process', *Palestine-Israel Journal*, Vol. 5.

Arnon, A. and Bamya, S. (2010) 'Economic Dimensions of a Two-State Agreement Between Israel and Palestine', *AIX Group*. Vol. II: Supplementary Papers.

B'Tselem. (2004) 'Facing the Abyss: The Isolation of Sheikh Sa'ad Village – Before and After the Separation Barrier', *B'Tselem*.

B'Tselem. (2005) 'Under the Guise of Security: Routing the Separation Barrier to Enable the Expansion of Israeli Settlements in the West Bank', *B'Tselem, Bimkom*.

B'Tselem. (2007) 'Crossing the Line: Violation of the Rights of Palestinians in Israel without a Permit', *B'Tselem*.

B'Tselem. (2010) 'By Hook and By Crook: Israeli Settlement Policy in the West Bank', *B'Tselem*.

B'Tselem. (2011/2015 updated) 'Checkpoints, Physical Obstructions, and Forbidden Roads', *B'Tselem*.

B'Tselem. (2016) 'Palestinians Killed by Israeli Security Forces in the West Bank, After Operation Cast Lead', *B'Tselem Statistics.*

Bank of Israel. (2014) 'Bank of Israel Annual Report', *Bank of Israel*, pp. 137–165.

Bank of Israel. (2015) 'Preliminary Version – Bank of Israel Annual Report – 2015', *Bank of Israel.*

Benvenisti, E. (2012) *The International Law of Occupation.* Oxford University Press, Oxford.

Bishara, M. (2001) *Palestine/Israel: Peace or Apartheid: Prospects for Resolving the Conflict.* Zed Books, London.

Bonacich, E. (1972) A Theory of Ethnic Antagonism: the Split Labor Market. *American Sociological Review.* Vol. 37 (5), pp. 547–559.

Carton, J. (2015) 'Israel Escalates "Water-Apartheid" As Illegal Settlers Contaminate Palestinian Water', *The Emergency, Water, Sanitation, and Hygiene Group (EWASH).*

Cohen, G. (2016) 'Palestinian Laborers Banned From Working on West Bank Settlements', *Ha'aretz.*

Dearden, L. (2016) 'Tel Aviv Attack: Israeli Authorities Seal off West Bank and Gaza as UN Condemns "Collective Punishment" of Palestinians', *The Independent.*

Ellman, M. and Laacher, S. (2003) 'Migrant Workers in Israel – A Contemporary Form of Slavery', *Euro-Mediterranean Human Rights Network & International Federation for Human Rights.*

Farjoun, E. (1984) 'Palestinian Workers in Israel: A Reserve Army of Labour' in Ed: Rothschild, J. (Ed.) *Forbidden Agendas: Intolerance and Defiance in the Middle East.* Zed Books, London.

Farsakh, L. (2002) Palestinian Labor Flows to the Israeli Economy: A Finished Story?. *Journal of Palestine Studies,* Vol. 32 (1), pp. 13–27.

Firro, K. (1999) *The Druzes in the Jewish State: A Brief History.* Brill, Leiden.

Hachlili, N. (2015) 'How to Stop Palestinians Unionizing: Security, Security Security'. *+972 Magazine.*

Halper, J. (2000) 'The 94 Percent Solution: A Matrix of Control'. *Middle East Report*, No. 216.

Halper, J. and Schaeffer, E. (2012) 'Israel's Policy of Demolishing Homes Must End: A Submission to the UN Human Rights Council'. *The Israeli Committee Against House Demolitions.*

Hass, A. (2002) Israel's Closure Policy: An Ineffective Strategy of Containment and Repression. *Journal of Palestine Studies*, Vol. 31 (3), pp. 5–20.

Hass, A. (2016) 'Israel Dramatically Ramping Up Demolitions of Palestinians Homes in West Bank', *Ha'aretz*.

Heintz, J. (2006) Low-Wage Manufacturing and Global Commodity Chains: A Model in the Unequal Exchange Tradition. *Cambridge Journal of Economics*, Vol. 30 (4), pp. 507–520.

Hever, S. (2010) *The Political Economy of Israel's Occupation*. Pluto Press, London.

Human Rights Watch. (1996) Israel: Israel's Closure of the West Bank and Gaza Strip. *Human Rights Watch*, Vol. 8 (3).

Human Rights Watch. (2015) 'Israel: Settlement Agriculture Harms Palestinian Children. Out of School, Doing Risky Work for Low Pay', *Human Rights Watch*.

Human Rights Watch. (2016) 'Occupation Inc: How Settlement Businesses Contribute to Israel's Violations of Palestinian Rights'. *Human Rights Watch*.

Institut de Droit International. (2003) 'Bruges Declaration on the Use of Force', *Institut de Droit International*.

International Court of Justice. (2004) 'Advisory Opinion: Legal Consequences of the construction of a Wall in the Occupied Palestinian Territory', *International Court of Justice*.

International Criminal Tribunal for the former Yugoslavia. (2006) 'The Prosecutor v. Milomir Stakić'. T-97-24-T, Appeals Chamber, Judgment, 22.

International Labor Organization. (2008) 'Combating Forced Labour: A Handbook for Employers and Business', *International Labor Organization*.

International Labor Organization. (2012 [1930]) 'Forced Labour Convention, 1930 (No. 29)', *International Labor Organization*, Geneva, 14th ILC session.

International Labor Organization. (2015) 'The Situation of Workers of the Occupied Arab Territories', *International Labor Organization*, Report of the Director-General, International Labour Conference, 104th Session.

International Trade Union Confederation. (2008) 'Forced Labour: Mini Action Guide', *International Trade Union Confederation*.

Kanaaneh, R. (2009) *Surrounded: Palestinian Soldiers in the Israeli Military*. Stanford University Press, Stanford.

Kaplan, M. (2015) 'Israeli Civilians To Take Up Arms? Jerusalem Mayor Tells Citizens To Carry Weapons As Violence In City Continues To Soar', *International Business Times*.

Kav LaOved. (2009a) 'Palestinian Farm Workers in Settlements Poisoned by Pesticides', *Kav LaOved*.

Kav LaOved. (2009b) 'Palestinian Workers Hanging from Treetops in Jordan Valley Settlements', *Kav LaOved*.

Kav LaOved. (2012) 'Employment of Palestinians in Israel and the Settlements: Restrictive Policies and Abuse of Rights'. *Kav LaOved*.

Kav LaOved. (2013) 'Non-Enforcement of the Law on Israeli Employers in the Occupied Territories: A Selective List of Israeli Companies Violating Palestinian Workers' Rights', *Kav LaOved*.

Kav LaOved. (2016) 'Palestinian Workers: Background, Challenges, Achievements', *Kav LaOved*.

Khalel, S. and Vickery, M. (2015) 'Israel's Dirty Secret: Inhumane Conditions for Thai Workers', *The Middle East Eye*, Published 2014, Updated 2015.

Khoury, J. Issacharoff, A. Pfeffer, A. (2011) 'Palestinian Authority Closely Coordinating Security Operations With Israel', *Ha'aretz*.

Levinson, C. (2013) 'Just 0.7% of State Land in the West Bank Has Been Allocated to Palestinians, Israel Admits', *Ha'aretz*.

Levinson, C., Lis, J. and Ravid, B. (2013) 'With Peace Talks Underway: Israel Planning to Construct Some 20,000 Housing Units in West Bank', *Ha'aretz*.

Lustick, I. (1980) *Arabs in the Jewish State – Israel's Control of a National Minority*. University of Texas Press, Austin.

Ma'an News Agency. (2015) 'Israeli Water Company Cuts Supply to Northern West Bank Villages', *Ma'an News Agency*.

Machsom Watch. (2007) 'Invisible Prisoners – Palestinians blacklisted by the General Security Services', *Machsom Watch*.

Marx, K. (1990 [1867]) *Das Kapital: Capital Volume I*. Penguin Books, London.

Marx, K. and Engels, F. (2010. [1848]) *The Communist Manifesto*. Vintage, London.

Melon, M. (2012) The Forcible Transfer of the Palestinian People from the Jordan Valley. *Al-Majdal*, BADIL Resource Center for Palestinian Residency and Refugee Rights, pp. 28–33.

Miaari, H. S., Zussman, A. and Zussman, N. (2010) 'Ethnic Conflict and Job Separations', *Households in Conflict Network*, HiCN Working Papers 76.

Ministerial Committee for Security Affairs. (1970) *Resolution No. B/1*.

National Insurance Institute of Israel. (2015) 'Information – Minimum Wage', *State of Israel*.

Office for the Coordination of Humanitarian Affairs. (2010) 'Special Focus: The Impact of the Barrier on Health', *United Nations*.

Office for the Coordination of Humanitarian Affairs. (2011) 'Barrier Update', *United Nations.*

Office for the Coordination of Humanitarian Affairs. (2012) 'The Humanitarian Impact of the Barrier', *United Nations.*

Office for the Coordination of Humanitarian Affairs. (2014a) 'Area C of the West Bank: Key Humanitarian Concerns', *United Nations.*

Office for the Coordination of Humanitarian Affairs. (2014b) 'Fragmented Lives: Humanitarian Overview', *United Nations.*

Office for the Coordination of Humanitarian Affairs. (2014c) 'East Jerusalem: Key Humanitarian Concerns', *United Nations.*

Office for the Coordination of Humanitarian Affairs. (2016) 'Press Release: Humanitarian Coordination Calls on Israel to Halt Demolitions in the Occupied West Bank Immediately and to Respect International Law', *United Nations.*

Palestine Ministry of Finance. (2014) 'Fiscal Operations', *Palestinian Authority.*

Pappe, I. (2011) *The Forgotten Palestinians: A History of the Palestinians in Israel.* Yale University Press, London.

Peace Now. (2015) 'Netanyahu Established 20 New Settlements for Tens of Thousands of Settlers', *Peace Now.*

Peck, J. (1989) Reconceptualizing the local labour market: Space, segmentation, and the state. *Progress in Human Geography,* Vol. 13, pp. 42–61.

Ravid, B. (2015) 'Netanyahu Approves 454 New Housing Units Beyond Green Line', *Ha'aretz.*

Reich, M., Gordon, D. and Edwards, R. (1973) A Theory of Labor Market Segmentation. *American Economic Review,* Vol. 63 (2), pp. 359–365.

Rettig Gur. (2014) 'Study Finds Huge Wage Gap Between Ashkenazim, Mizrahim', *The Times of Israel.*

Rosenhek, Z. (2003) The Political Dynamics of a Segmented Labour Market: Palestinian Citizens, Palestinians from the Occupied Territories and Migrant Workers in Israel. *Acta Sociologica* Vol. 46 (3), pp. 231–249.

Roy, S. (2001) Palestinian Society and Economy: The Continued Denial of Possibility. *Journal of Palestine Studies,* Vol. 30 (4), pp. 5–20.

Samara, A. (1988) *The Political Economy of the West Bank 1967–1987, From Peripheralization to Development.* Khamsin, Paris.

Samara, A. (2000) Globalisation, the Palestinian Economy, and the "Peace Process". *Journal of Palestine Studies.* Vol. 29 (2), pp. 20–34.

Sason, T. (2005) 'Summary of the Opinion Concerning Unauthorized Outposts – Talya Sason, Adv.', *Israel Ministry of Foreign Affairs.*

Sbeih, M. (2011) 'Palestinian Wage Workers in Israeli Settlements in the West Bank – Characteristics and Work Circumstances', *The Democracy and Workers' Rights Center*, Unpublished.

Shafir, G. (1989) *Land, Labor and the Origins of the Israeli-Palestinian Conflict.* Cambridge University Press, Cambridge.

State Comptroller. (2011) *Annual Report*, No. 62.

State Comptroller. (2013) *Annual Report*, No. 63b.

State Comptroller. (2014) *Annual Report*, No. 64.

Stork, J. (1983) Water and Israel's Occupation Strategy. *Middle East Report*, Vol. 13 (116).

Swisher, C. (2011) *The Palestine Papers: The End of the Road.* Hesperus Press, London.

The Rights Forum and Yesh Din. (2015) 'Under the Radar: Israel's silent policy of transforming unauthorized outposts into official settlements', *The Rights Forum and Yesh Din.*

United Nations. (2013 [1948]) 'The Universal Declaration of Human Rights', *United Nations.*

United Nations Relief and Works Agency. (2016) 'Relief & Social Services', *United Nations.*

Vickery, M. (2016a) 'Thai Farmworkers in Israel Suffer Labor Abuses', *USA Today.*

Vickery, M. (2016b) 'The Hotbed of Hopelessness', *Sunday Herald.*

Weizman, E. (2007) *Hollow Land: Israel's Architecture of Occupation.* Verso, London.

White, B. (2011) *Palestinians in Israel: Segregation, Discrimination and Democracy.* Pluto Press, London.

Who Profits. (2012) 'Palestinian Workers in Settlements: Who Profits' Position Paper'. *Who Profits.*

Wolf, A.T. (1995) *Hydropolitics Along the Jordan River: Scarce Water and its Impact on the Arab-Israeli Confict.* United Nations University Press, Tokyo.

World Bank. (2008) 'West Bank and Gaza. Palestinian Trade: West Bank Routes', *World Bank*, Report No. 46807 – GZ.

World Bank. (2012) 'Fiscal Crisis, Economic Prospects: The Imperative for Economic Cohesion in the Palestinian Territories', *World Bank.*

World Bank. (2013) 'Area C and the Future of the Palestinian Economy', *World Bank.*

Index

wages, 43, 122–3; minimum *see*
minimum wage; of Israeli
workers, 52; of middlemen, 26;
of Palestinian civil servants,
unpaid, 85; of Palestinian
workers, 57 (low, 2, 3, 11, 26, 40,
47, 48, 51, 64, 73, 113, 119)
Wall, 17, 49, 50, 51, 92, 93, 94–5,
97; building of, 5, 15; crossing
of, 12
water: access to, 37, 87; Israeli
control of, 48; reservoirs of, 37–8
West Bank: economy of,
described as unsustainable, 88;
fragmentation of, 96; labour
segregation in, 77–80; splitting
of, 87
Who Profits research center, 123
women, Palestinian, work of, 42,
113
work permits, 11, 92, 106;

conditions for, 107; destroyed
by soldiers, 61; employers'
exploitation of, 13; employers'
interest in, 110; faking of, 28; for
work in Israel, 115; power of,
21–9; rescinding of, 22; system
of, 79–80, 116 (manipulated by
state, 115); termination of, 62;
working without, 12
working hours, false reporting of,
66
World Bank, 86, 88
World Health Organization
(WHO), 37

Yafit settlement, 32
Yazan, a teenager, 32, 33–6, 39

Zacharia, a teenager, 42, 43–4
Zionism, 78, 81
Zubeidat, Hamza, 30